Play Classical Guitar

David Braid

Classical guitar construction is based on a long tradition handed down by generations of Spanish luthiers, dating back to legends of the 19th century like Antonio de Torres, and even earlier craftsmen.

In  dvances in available ...emands of modern ...ead of new construction ...e, the United States,

...ument, basic designs ...alike at first glance, but the difference – and the resulting quality of sound and playability – is in the detail.

This page shows an "exploded" view of a classical guitar, to give an idea of its construction.

The BACK of the guitar is bookmatched (like the soundboard, see above right) – though in this case made from a hardwood such as rosewood or mahogany. The two halves are then braced from the inside with either three or (in some modern guitars) four transverse bars. The back is actually the last part to be attached during construction (despite how this diagram appears). The RIBS, or sides of the guitars are also cut from sheets of hardwood, but are heated and bent to shape. They're then joined at the bottom, where they're glued to an END BLOCK – a piece of light hardwood (willow, lime, poplar). At the top they slot into the end of the neck. The narrowest point of the body is called the WAIST and the upper and lower sections called BOUTS.

The modern BRIDGE, with detachable SADDLE (traditionally bone or ivory), is one of the most recent elements of the classical guitar, introduced in the 1850s. Rosewood is the usual bridge material, and here its elegance is enhanced by MARQUETRY to match the design of the ROSETTE – the often complex decorative mosaic around the SOUNDHOLE that's one of a guitar-maker's trademarks.

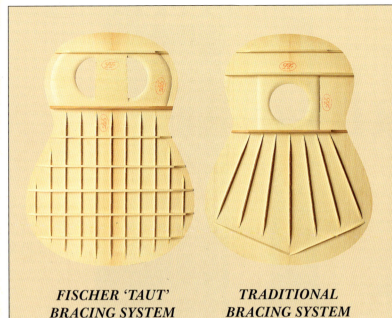

FISCHER 'TAUT' BRACING SYSTEM   **TRADITIONAL BRACING SYSTEM**

The SOUNDBOARD is the top surface of a classical guitar, and is the single most important element in determining the sound quality of the instrument. A piece of spruce or cedar is "bookmatched" – sliced in half laterally and the halves glued side-by-side so the grain matches – then carefully braced internally to stiffen without adding too much extra weight.

The soundboard on the right of this pair shows the traditional Torres bracing system: seven light "fan-struts" pointing at the 12th fret. To its left is UK luthier Paul Fischer's TAUT system: this criss-cross lattice of lightweight spruce allows more design scope, like a thinner soundboard and reconfigured soundhole.

The NECK (traditionally wider and flatter than most other types of guitar neck) is cut to shape from a length of hardwood. To achieve its backwards slope, the HEAD is usually sawn from the top of the neck wood with a diagonal cut, turned over and glued back on. It's then veneered and holes drilled for the machineheads (string-tuning mechanisms). The HEEL (the visible joint with the body) and the FOOT (the interior part of the joint) are built up from several layers of the same wood. The FINGERBOARD is cut (from ebony or rosewood) before fitting to the neck. Nickel-silver FRETS are then hammered into place. The NUT is traditionally a slotted piece of bone which guides the strings at the top of the neck.

The STRINGS themselves are nowadays nylon (originally animal gut), with the three bass strings wound in wire, and are available in various "tensions" – high tension delivers a brighter, livelier tone, but is harder on the fingers. The strings are traditionally tied at the bridge. The wood strips seen here with the regular cuts across them are flexible KERFED LININGS, which reinforce the joint between sides, front and back. The narrower strips are PURFLINGS, which are inlaid into the guitar body at various points for decorative purposes.

Play Classical Guitar
By David Braid

A BACKBEAT BOOK
First edition 2001

Published by Backbeat Books
600 Harrison Street,
San Francisco, CA 94107, USA
www.backbeatbooks.com

An imprint of The Music Player Network CMP Media LLC.

Published for Backbeat Books by Outline Press Ltd,
Unit 2a Union Court, 20-22 Union Road,
Clapham, London SW4 6JP, England.
www.backbeatuk.com

Copyright © 2001 Balafon. All rights reserved.
No part of this book covered by the copyrights hereon may be reproduced or copied in any manner whatsoever without written permission, except in the case of brief quotations embodied in articles or reviews where the source should be made clear.
For more information contact the publishers.

ISBN 13: 978-0-87930-657-1
ISBN 10: 0-87930-657-2

Printed in Hong Kong

Art Director: Nigel Osborne
Editorial Director: Tony Bacon
Design: Paul Cooper
Editor: Paul Quinn
Production: Phil Richardson
Model: Helen Sanderson
Photography: Chris Christodoulou

Recording details
Sound Engineer: John Taylor
Location: Holy Trinity Church, Weston, Hertfordshire
Guitar: James Baker, 1997

Origination by Global Colour (Malaysia)

08 09 10 11 6 5 4 3

contents

SECTION ONE

Playing position	6
Check points	7
Tuning using the fifth fret	8
Finger and thumb strokes	10
Tirando	10
Apoyando	11
Right-hand chord	12
Arpeggios	13
Notation	14
Note values	14
Time signatures	15
Guitar notation	15
Right hand exercises	16
Introducing the left hand	18
The note C	19
The note D	20
Pieces with A, C and D	22
$\frac{3}{4}$ Time	23
Open bass strings	24
Rests	26
Two part music	26
Notes F and G	27
Ties	28
Anacrusis	29

SECTION TWO

Quavers (eighth-notes)	32
Sharp sign: ♯	33
$\frac{2}{4}$ time	34
The note A	34
Dotted rhythm	35
Key signatures	36
E & F on the fourth string	37
Intervals	39
Notes B and C	40
Counterpoint	41
Dynamics	42
F & G on the sixth string	45
$\frac{6}{8}$ time	46
Semiquavers (16th-notes)	48
Flat sign: ♭	51

SECTION THREE

Memorisation	56
Tempo	58
Dynamics – part two	58
Intervals – part two	61
Legato	62
Second position (II)	64
Order of sharps and flats	66
Irrational rhythms	68
Arpeggios – part two	70
Melody within arpeggio	72
Damping	73
Half-barre	75

SECTION FOUR

Ligado	78
Chords	79
Chord diagrams	80
Third position (III)	83
Octave shapes	83
Tempo – part two	84
The full barre	86
Ligado – part two	87
Fifth position (V)	88
Ornaments	90
Acciaccatura	90
Mordent	90
Appoggiatura	91
Turn	92
Trill	92

SECTION FIVE

Scales	95
Time signatures – part two	98
Seventh position (VII)	99
Glissando	100
Nails	101
Vibrato	102
Harmonics	104
Artificial harmonics	105
General musicianship	106
Sight-reading	108
Ninth position (IX)	108
Tremolo	110

SECTION SIX

Tone colour	117
Scales – part two	118
Demisemiquavers	121
Extended techniques	122
Pizzicato	122
Tambor	123
Bartók or snap pizz	123
Scodatura	123
Campanella	124
Four study pieces	124
History of repertoire	130
Buying an instrument	137
Glossary	140
CD track listing	144

Your audio CD can be found inside the back cover.

Play Classical Guitar

David Braid

This book can be used either by a student working alone or in conjunction with a guitar teacher. The accompanying CD will be particularly helpful to those learning on their own.

The teaching method revolves around selected pieces of music designed to cover elements of musical theory and practical playing technique. It's not necessary to read music already, as this is taught alongside the craft of playing the instrument itself. The techniques are those used in the main schools of classical guitar teaching, ranging from the basic arpeggio-based right-hand position to the skill of playing by ear. And throughout the book there are clear, explanatory diagrams.

The book's flexible approach will suit players of all standards and backgrounds – from school-age students learning their first instrument to experienced but non-reading guitarists from other styles of music who are interested in developing their technique and musicianship.

This book is dedicated to Charles Ramirez, my former teacher at the Royal College of Music in London.

PLAY CLASSICAL GUITAR
SECTION ONE

Playing position

Tuning using the fifth fret

Basic finger & thumb strokes

Right-hand chord & arpeggio

Musical & guitar notation

First exercises – right hand only

Introducing the left hand

The notes A, C, D, F & G

Simple time signatures

Two-part music: bass & treble lines

Rests, ties & anacrusis

SECTION ONE
PLAY CLASSICAL GUITAR

Playing position

The classical guitar-playing position stems directly from the practicalities of keeping the instrument steady while having the hands free to play (no supporting strap is used). The traditional position not only allows the left hand to move easily around the fingerboard, but also lets you make sudden right-hand position changes – perhaps from an arpeggio to a chord strum.

The left leg should be raised by using a small foot stool, or any suitable object (somewhere between five and nine inches high, depending on what feels most comfortable). The aim is to raise the guitar neck so all parts of the fingerboard can be reached easily, with the left hand just below shoulder height.

Without using the hands at all, the guitar should be supported in four places:

- Resting on the left thigh.
- Leaning against the right inner thigh.
- Underneath the right forearm (just below the elbow).
- The guitar back leaning on the left side of your chest.

Note: If you are one of the few people who have chosen to play the guitar left-handed, you should of course reverse all references to "left" and "right" in the book. In fact, it's much more common for naturally left-handed players to persevere with learning right-handed technique, thus avoiding problems of finding suitable instruments, or attempting to adapt often complex classical repertoire to suit.

The photo on the left shows both hand positions from the player's perspective. Note the small triangle formed by the right-hand thumb, index finger and strings: this position ensures the thumb and fingers keep out of each other's way, and can all play freely. To achieve this, the thumb always points left (towards the neck) and the fingers curve in the opposite direction, towards the bridge.

Check points:

- The shoulders and arms should be completely relaxed.
- The right hand falls naturally into place, just through gravity.
- The guitar neck should be angled so the left-hand fingers are easily visible. Since the aim is to be able to play most music from memory (see *Memorisation* in Section Three), you'll use your eyes to guide the left hand to its next position on the fretboard. (It's vital the eye moves first and the hand follows, not vice-versa.)
- Both thumbs should be in a natural, straight position, and fingers (on both hands) should be curved inwards.
- Try to keep a slight gap between the palm of the left hand and the neck of the guitar.

The four photographs across these pages show the ideal playing position from different angles. Note the completely relaxed shoulders, the vertical line of the lower left leg, and how the right leg makes room for the instrument. This ensures the guitar goes across the body, with the join between the guitar's neck and body directly above the left leg (making this a balanced mid-point). The last photograph shows the slight angle of the guitar body – this lets the player see the fingerboard clearly, and also greatly enhances sound projection.

PLAY CLASSICAL GUITAR

SECTION ONE
PLAY CLASSICAL GUITAR

Tuning using the fifth fret

The traditional way to tune a guitar is by taking the note A from a tuning fork, pitch pipe or piano, and then making sure the guitar's top E-string is in tune (holding the fifth fret, as shown below).

To tune the other strings you have to find the equivalent notes to the open strings. On the second (B) string, the fifth fret will give you the same E note as the open first string (as you can see on the guitar neck opposite).

If the B-string isn't in tune, this note will be either higher or lower in pitch than the open-string E. Turn the relevant machinehead (tuning peg) to tune the B-string to the correct pitch (see the diagram on the next page – or just follow the string along to the machinehead if you're not sure which one to turn).

Turning the machinehead *away* from the neck (looking from the playing side, or *clockwise* viewed from the front) will tighten the string, taking it up in pitch. Turning it *towards* the neck (*counter-clockwise* viewed from the front) will take the string down in pitch.

Once the B-string is in tune, do the same thing for the other strings – with the important exception that on the *third* string, the note that matches the open second string is at the *fourth* fret rather than the fifth (again, see diagram on the opposite page).

The rest of the strings are tuned in the same way as the second string was, using the fifth fret to match the previous open string.

The picture below shows the notes on the piano that correspond to the open strings on the guitar. Notice that the G and B are only four notes apart, while all the others are five apart - this helps show why the second string (B) is tuned using the fourth fret of the third-string (G), rather than the fifth. If you read music already, you'll be aware that the notes on the keyboard seem to be an octave lower than those written in guitar music – this is because the guitar is a "transposing instrument", and sounds an octave lower than written.

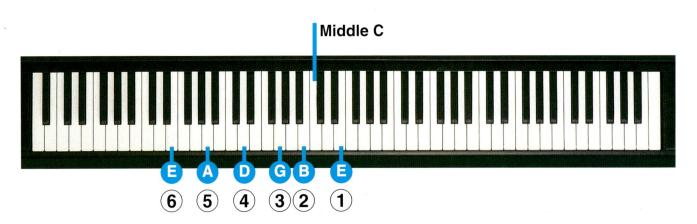

This picture shows an A note on the guitar neck that corresponds to a "concert pitch" (440Hz) tuning fork.

SECTION ONE
PLAY CLASSICAL GUITAR

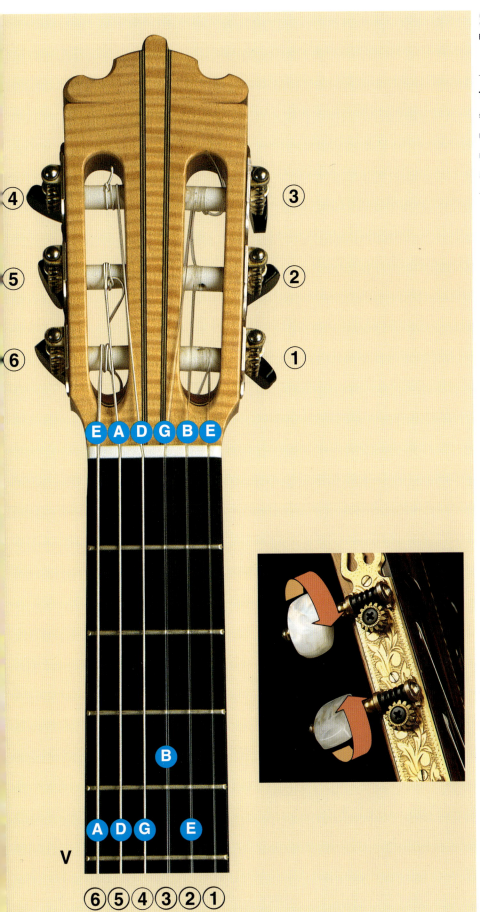

The guitar neck picture on this page shows the string numbers and their relevant machineheads, and also the notes used for tuning from string to string (at frets IV and V).

The top arrow shows the direction of the machinehead "button" for loosening the string – turning down towards the neck – to lower its pitch. The bottom arrow shows the reverse – rotating the machinehead up and away from the neck, to raise the string's pitch.

PLAY CLASSICAL GUITAR

SECTION ONE
PLAY CLASSICAL GUITAR

Basic finger & thumb strokes

There are two main types of finger stroke in classical guitar-playing: "tirando", also known as free stroke; and "apoyando", or rest stroke. Tirando is the stroke you'll use most of the time – it makes it easy to play several strings at once, and lets neighbouring strings ring where required. Apoyando is generally used to accentuate certain notes or phrases.

Tirando

The thumb and fingers of the right hand should always work in opposite directions to each other. The thumb moves slightly away from the guitar after playing and makes a small circle, returning to the string for the next stroke (see photographs below).

The fingers move primarily from the knuckle joint and have little movement in the first and second joints. They play into the hand, following-through upwards and past the string.

In order for the thumb and fingers to work freely, they must be kept slightly apart from each other, with the thumb pointing leftwards and the fingers angled to the right (see photo on p7).

Photos 1 & 2 on this page show the preparation and execution of tirando with the index finger: note the finger moves into the hand, playing the string then following through afterwards. Photos 3 & 4 show the preparation and movement of the thumb when playing tirando: the thumb moves downwards and then out from the string

Apoyando

Apoyando is when the finger or thumb comes to rest on an adjacent string after playing, and is used when a particularly rounded sound is required with a bit of extra weight. This may be in single line themes or on notes or phrases that need to be highlighted and brought out over the other parts.

Apoyando with the thumb is achieved by slightly adjusting the angle of playing so the thumb moves downwards and comes to rest briefly on the next string.

There are two ways of playing apoyando with the fingers. The most common is when the first joint of the finger "gives way" (bends backwards slightly) as it plays the string, allowing the fingertip to pass easily over the string to rest on the next one. The tone produced is characteristically sweet and rich.

The other type of apoyando is when the first joint doesn't move, remaining stiff, which produces a slightly harder, percussive attack. The latter is often used by flamenco players and is good for very fast playing of scale-like passages.

The series of photographs below will make the difference between apoyando and tirando clear.

Photos 1 & 2 on this page show the position of the index finger before and after an apoyando stroke. In photo 1, note that the hand is slightly higher up the strings and the finger is much less curved than when playing tirando. Photo 2 shows the final resting place of the finger on the next string (in this case the second-string, B).

Photos 3 & 4 on this page show the apoyando thumb stroke. Note that the hand is considerably lower in relation to the strings than when playing tirando. As with the finger apoyando, the thumb rests on the next string after the stroke.

SECTION ONE
PLAY CLASSICAL GUITAR

Right-hand chord

In classical guitar-playing, the right-hand fingers are identified by using the letters **p**, **i**, **m** and **a** – these must be memorised so they can be identified instantly on a musical score. The letters come from their Spanish names:

p for **pulgar** – thumb
i for **indice** – index (first) finger
m for **medio** – middle (second) finger
a for **anular** – ring (third) finger

The fourth finger on the right hand is never used – especially not for leaning on the soundboard, as this can restrict the movement of the third finger.

The basic position of the right hand on the guitar can be located and established through the use of what's called the "right-hand chord" – see photo 1 below.

To begin with, **p** rests on the fourth string (D), **i** on the third string (G), **m** on the second (B), and **a** on the first string (E). This "prepared" chord can be seen as a kind of home position from which all other right-hand technique is developed.

The thumb and fingers must play exactly together, and each string should be clearly heard and balanced in volume. This may seem a bit difficult when you first attempt it, but if the fingers and thumb are "prepared" on the strings beforehand, the correct movement will be easier.

It's important to keep the thumb away from the fingers, gently drawing the fingers into the hand while pushing the thumb outwards (see photo 2 below).

The hand itself should hardly move at all – this may also be tricky at first, but think of your right hand as a balanced mid-point from which the thumb and fingers operate as they move around in opposite directions.

Photo 1 here shows the ideal preparation for the right-hand chord. Note the angle of the fingers and straight shape of the thumb. In photo 2 the finger & thumb movement has been completed, but the hand is still in the same place, allowing for an immediate repetition.

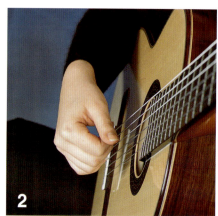

Arpeggios

A half-arpeggio is prepared in the same way as the chord but the thumb and fingers play one after the other rather than simultaneously.

The thumb begins and is followed by the **i** finger on G, the **m** on B and **a** on E, making sure the fingers are moved from the knuckle and are directed into the hand. It's best to practise the arpeggio several times in a row with no break in-between, so there's a continuous cycle.

For the second and subsequent arpeggios the fingers aren't prepared on the strings, as this would stop the previous notes ringing.

The full arpeggio is similar to the half but has six notes, returning to the beginning by adding two further strokes on the B and G strings with **m** and **i** respectively. The complete arpeggio is: **p**, **i**, **m**, **a**, **m**, **i**, on strings D, G, B, E, B, G.

This can be developed further by moving the thumb to the fifth string (A) the next time round and then on to the 6th string (E), then back via the A to the D to begin again.

These five photos show the preparation for the arpeggio and subsequent movement of the thumb and three fingers. Note that the fingers that are yet to play stay firmly on the string until they are needed – this is very important, ensuring no time is lost looking for the string.

SECTION ONE
PLAY CLASSICAL GUITAR

Notation

Musical notation is written on a grid of five horizontal lines called a "stave" (or staff). Each line and each space on the stave represents a note of a different pitch, named after the first seven letters of the alphabet: A, B, C, D, E, F, G. After this the notes start repeating in a higher or lower "octave" – an octave is so-called because there are eight main steps from one note to its equivalent note, above or below.

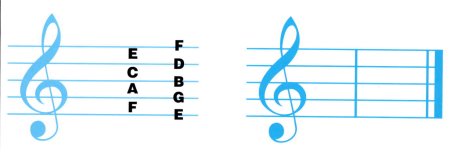

The symbol at the beginning of the stave is called a clef. There are several types of clef, but this one, a treble clef, is really the only one you will come across as a guitarist (other clefs, such as the bass clef, show different parts of the musical range).

The notes on the lines of the treble clef stave are, from the bottom: E, G, B, D, F (it may help you remember this order if you make up a mnemonic using these letters - a common one is Every Good Boy Deserves Fun). The notes in the spaces, going up, are: F, A, C, E. When notes are used that go outside the range of the stave (either above or below), short lines called "ledger lines" – long enough for just one note – are added to extend the stave.

Most music is divided into bars, as shown in the second diagram above, by vertical "barlines" which group the music into equal sections to make it easier to read. Although the bars divide the music evenly according to the time signature they are not to be heard as such – you mustn't pause or stop at each barline. A double barline indicates the end of the piece of music.

Note values

The notes themselves can last for different lengths of time, as indicated by symbols called note values. At this stage we'll only deal with the three main types:

The crotchet (quarter note) – ♩ *(note stems can go up or down)*

The minim (half note) – ♩

The semibreve (whole note) – 𝅝

Time signatures

The type and amount of note values in each bar (and therefore the pulse of the piece) is indicated at the beginning of the music by the "time signature". This consists of two small numbers arranged vertically (for instance 4/4).

The top digit indicates the number of notes (or beats) per bar and the lower number indicates the note value itself, which is represented by its fraction of a semibreve (whole note). So, for example, the crotchet (quarter note) is indicated by the lower number 4; the minim (half note) by a 2; and the semibreve (whole note) by a 1.

The most frequently used time signature is 4/4 – four crotchets in a bar – often called "common time", and sometimes indicated by just a capital C at the start of the passage, instead of the two fours. Other frequently used time signatures are 2/4 and 3/4, which will be dealt with in greater detail in the first two Sections in the book.

Guitar notation

As well as the standard musical notation, there are some additional signs specific to written guitar music:

A number from 1-4, written above or under a note on the stave, indicates which left-hand finger is to be used to hold down that note on the fingerboard. (If the number 0 appears, the open string is to be played.)

A number in a circle (for instance ⑥) indicates which string is to be played.

Roman numerals (I, II, III, IV, V etc) indicate the fret position at which to hold down the notes (we'll go into this in more detail later).

The letters **p**, **i**, **m** and **a** (as mentioned on p12) on the stave refer to the right-hand fingering. Just to remind you:

p for **pulgar** – thumb
i for **indice** – index (first) finger
m for **medio** – middle (second) finger
a for **anular** – ring (third) finger

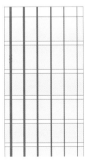

Guitar chords, as we'll see in Section Four, are sometimes notated on a "chord diagram" – a grid representing the guitar fingerboard, as if viewing the neck vertically, with the nut at the top and the low E-string on the left. The notes to be held down to make up the chord are usually indicated by black dots at the relevant frets.

SECTION ONE
PLAY CLASSICAL GUITAR

First exercises – right hand only

It's crucial, when working through the exercises in the book, that you do so at your own pace – repeat an exercise as many times as necessary until you've understood all its component elements completely. This will make the later pieces easier to grasp.

Always count the beats regularly, either out loud or in your mind, as this will help you keep a steady pulse. In the first three exercises the beats are written below the music as a guide.

Play quite slowly at first, paying close attention to hand position, fingering and note changes. Exercises 1 to 6 use only the right hand, so you can practise alternating the fingers.

When crossing from one string to another you mustn't hesitate or stop. Try not to look at the right hand – you want it to develop touch-sensitivity to the strings. Play these exercises using tirando (see p10) and rest the thumb on a bass string to steady the hand.

EXERCISE 1 *Using the open first and second strings only – changing strings between each bar, and mid-bar three. Remember not to look at the right hand.*

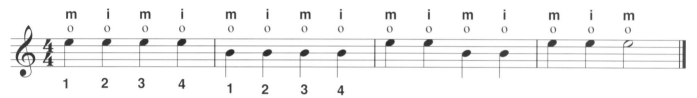

EXERCISE 2 *The third string, G, is introduced in bars two and three. Where the right-hand fingering is only given for one bar, it carries on in the same sequence.*

EXERCISE 3 *The third finger (**a**) joins the second (**m**) and first (**i**): **a** is used for three-note patterns, minimising hand movement by arpeggio-type fingering, such as the last three notes.*

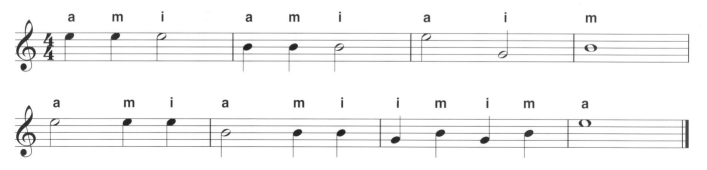

Here the rhythmic pattern, which lasts for two bars, is repeated three times, with different pitches each time. **EXERCISE 4**

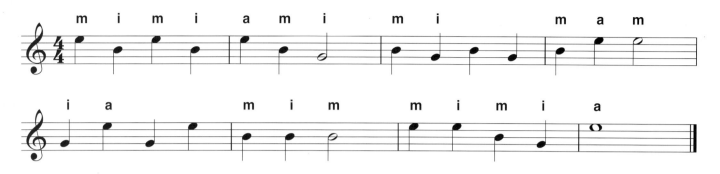

Again, a rhythmic pattern of two bars is repeated three times. **EXERCISE 5**

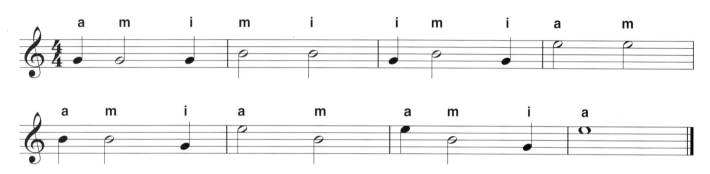

This one has a pattern of three within the beat of four. If learned carefully it can be sped up and the pattern will be clearly heard. The fingering is arpeggio-based with a separate finger for each string. **EXERCISE 6**

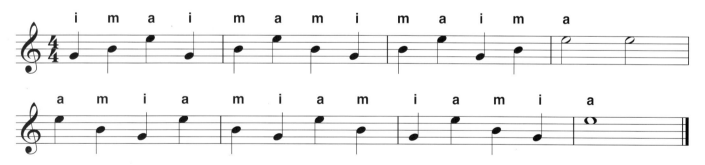

SECTION ONE
PLAY CLASSICAL GUITAR

Introducing the left hand

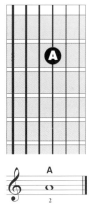

The left-hand fingers should always be as vertical as possible coming down on to the strings, so it's the fingertips that hold down the notes. The left-hand thumb must be held straight and should stay on the back of the neck directly opposite the second finger (in a line with the centre of the palm). Be careful the thumb doesn't creep over the top of the neck, as this would restrict finger movement. When you're learning you should always look at the left hand and the fretboard when not looking at the music – in contrast to the right hand, which will develop better if it's not watched. The first note to learn in the left hand is A on the third string, second fret, which is played with finger 2 (as in the diagram above).

EXERCISE 7 *This uses only the two notes of A and G on the same string.*

EXERCISE 8 *Introducing a third note, the open-string B, in bar four.*

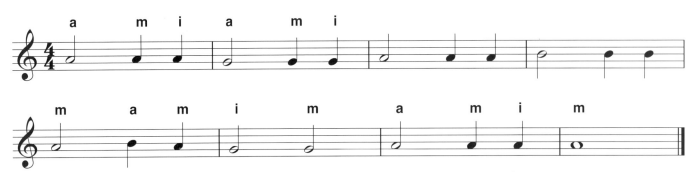

Pay close attention to the right-hand fingering here – it'll make string-crossing easier.

EXERCISE 9

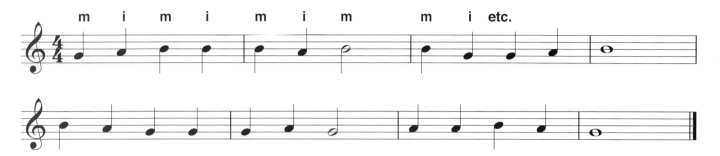

The note C

This note can be slightly more difficult than A at first – it's positioned closer to the nut, where the strings are more taut and it can be a bit harder to hold the notes down if you're new to using the left hand. Don't worry, strength will soon build up in the fingers – and the fingertips will toughen up with time. It's a good idea if the finger is put down on the string slowly to begin with, to help keep the hand more relaxed – don't grab at the notes. And remember to keep the thumb straight on the back of the neck, nearly opposite the fretting finger, for added support.

Remember to look at the fret you're moving to, rather than the finger itself.

EXERCISE 10

This exercise brings in the note G in bar three.

EXERCISE 11

SECTION ONE
PLAY CLASSICAL GUITAR

Exercise 12 uses left-hand notes A and C. When crossing strings, both left and right hand must change together (going to the A in bar one, for example). Remember to watch the left hand and never the right.

EXERCISE 12 *Try to memorise then play this exercise without the music. This makes you use your eyes to help the left hand find the notes on the correct strings.*

The note D

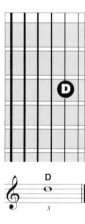

You should find this one a bit easier, having already done A and C – it's a little further up the neck, where the strings feel slightly looser. The downside is you have to hold it with the third finger, which is usually much weaker than the first two. Remember to keep the fingers curved inwards when they come down on the strings – if they're straight, or even bent back, they have that much less strength and manoeuvrability. Even though you've moved up to the third fret, keep the thumb roughly where it was, in line with fingers one or two, straight and strong on the back of the neck.

EXERCISE 13 *This is all on the second string - C and D only.*

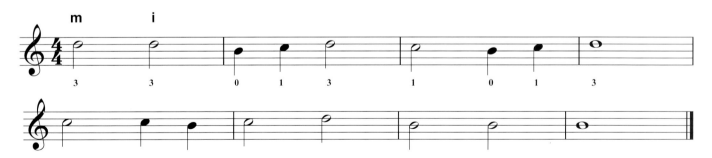

A folk song – it makes use of all six notes learned so far.   **EXERCISE 14**

'Twinkle Twinkle Little Star' – note the instruction "da capo al fine" at the end: this means you play to end of the piece once, return to the beginning, and repeat from the beginning as far as the word "fine" (which is Italian for "end"). This instruction is often written as DC al fine.   **EXERCISE 15**

SECTION ONE
PLAY CLASSICAL GUITAR

Pieces with A, C and D

Using these three left-hand notes in the same pieces is an important step – nearly all your playing later on will involve the left hand, with only the occasional open-string. Again it must be stressed that watching your left hand will assist your movements considerably as well as focusing your concentration.

EXERCISE 16 *The initial difficulty in this 'Folk Dance' is the jump from one left-hand note to another: C to A at the beginning and in bar two of line three. This movement must be practised separately and slowly until it feels comfortable.*

EXERCISE 17 *A scale study, which makes use of the first six notes in the scale of G (dealt with in full later in the book). Play this exercise using apoyando.*

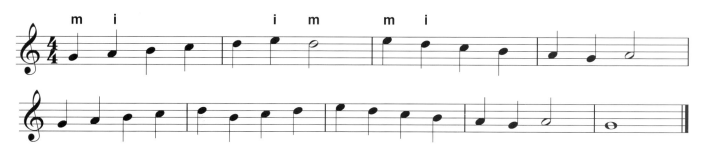

3/4 Time

In 3/4 time, as in 4/4, the unit of the beat is still a crotchet (the 4 at the bottom means we are dealing in quarter notes). The difference in 3/4 is there are now only three crotchets per bar instead of four. The use of 3/4 time, as with many time signatures, derives from dance rhythms – in this case the likes of the waltz, chaconne and much of flamenco. Although the natural stress of the bar falls on the first beat, this must not be accented, as it can make the music sound rather heavy.

SECTION ONE
PLAY CLASSICAL GUITAR

Notice the dot after the last note – this indicates the note has been lengthened by half its value. In this case, half the value (of the minim) is a crotchet, which when added on makes a note worth three beats rather than two: in other words, a note which lasts for the entire three-beat bar.

EXERCISE 18

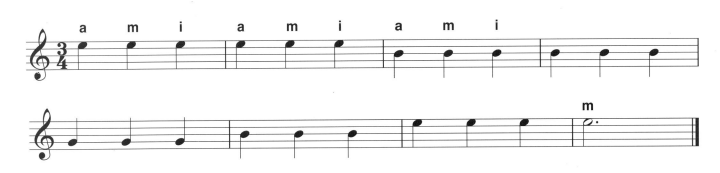

Watch for the right-hand pattern change in the penultimate bar. **EXERCISE 19**

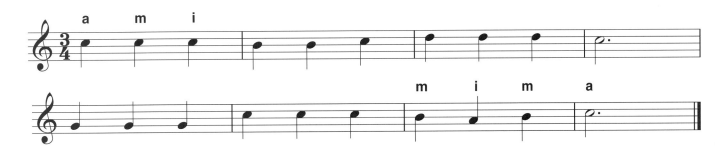

SECTION ONE
PLAY CLASSICAL GUITAR

EXERCISE 20 *This piece is made up of four phrases of four bars each. The third phrase, at the start of line two, is an exact repeat of the first.*

EXERCISE 21 *The C in the first bar here should be held right up till the D in bar two, so it sounds together with the E to create a passing harmony. Make sure the first finger comes onto the string vertically enough to avoid making contact with, and so damping, the open E.*

Open bass strings

The three bass strings (four, five and six) are nearly always played with the right-hand thumb (**p**). This leaves the fingers free to play the treble strings at the same time.

To help you remember the notation of the bass strings, note that the A has the second ledger line going right through it, and the E is directly below the third ledger line.

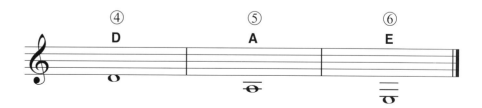

*When playing the open bass strings in Exercises 22-25 (with **p**), rest the other fingers on either the first string or the top three strings.*   **EXERCISE 22**

First two bars are the same rhythm – in bar three the rhythm is reversed.   **EXERCISE 23**

Note the different time signature. Keep beat steady when crossing strings.   **EXERCISE 24**

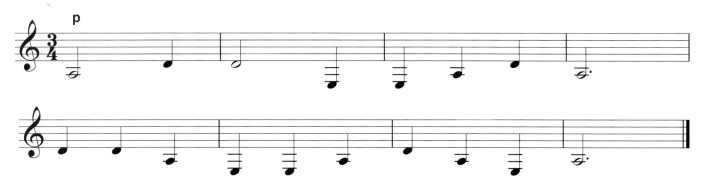

More string-jumping here: keep movements smooth; don't watch the thumb.   **EXERCISE 25**

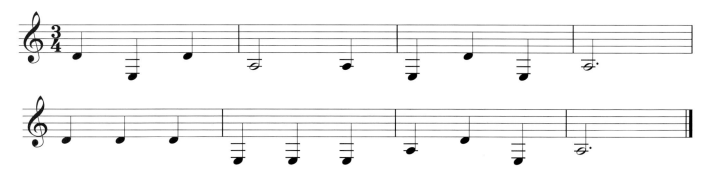

SECTION ONE
PLAY CLASSICAL GUITAR

Rests

Rests are used to provide a break or silence in one or several parts of the music. We'll deal with three types of rest at this point in the book, corresponding to the note values learnt so far:

The crotchet ♩ (quarter-note) rest = 𝄽

The minim 𝅗𝅥 (half-note) rest = ▬

The semibreve 𝅝 (whole-note) rest = ▬

The semibreve rest is also used to indicate a whole bar rest, irrespective of time signature. Here's how rests might be used:

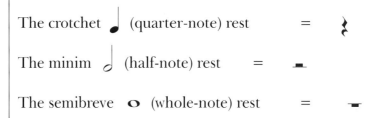

Two-part music – bass & treble

In most music, notes from the upper and lower ranges of the stave are combined within a piece to create a fuller listening experience. We'll start with simple, alternating bass and treble parts.

EXERCISE 26 *The semibreve rests here are used to keep the upper and lower parts of the music separate in time. The small curved lines next to some of the notes mean these are to be left to ring on – this means you can't keep resting the thumb on a bass string while playing the treble (or vice versa) as it will cut the ringing note abruptly short.*

EXERCISE 27 *At the end of this piece you'll see a repeat sign (two dots and a double bar line) – this means you repeat the whole piece. If there is another repeat sign, this time facing forward, then only the section between the two signs is to be repeated (this is shown in Exercise 28, on the next page).*

The second line is repeated note the symbols at the start and end of the line **EXERCISE 28**

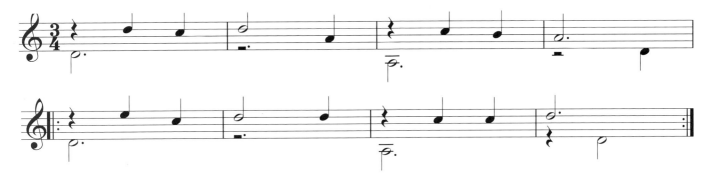

Notes F and G

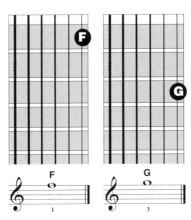

Not unlike playing the second-string notes C and D, except these are on the first string. This means we've now covered two G notes, which are an octave apart. If you play every note learnt so far, from the open third-string G up to this top-string G, you'll hear the eight notes in this octave. In bar six, be careful to make a smooth transition from the F on the first string to the D on the second string, as there's no open-string in-between to make this easier..

This works best at a quick, steady tempo – watch out for those changes from F to D (bars two and three of line two), where it's easy to slow down unintentionally. **EXERCISE 29**

SECTION ONE
PLAY CLASSICAL GUITAR

EXERCISE 30 *Here, some notes of the bass and treble parts are played simultaneously (see bars one & three). Start by just practising the high E and bass A in bar one on their own, until you can play them exactly together. Remember that the right-hand thumb and fingers must be kept apart and moved in opposite directions so they have space to operate freely.*

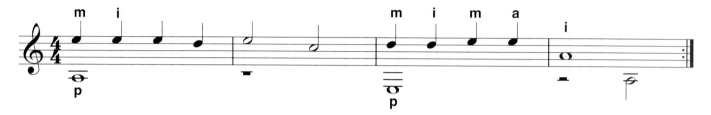

EXERCISE 31 *Keep the bass notes fairly subdued here so they don't overpower the top part.*

Ties

A tie is a curved line between two notes of the same pitch. It means the second note is not to be played but just held for the length of its value (so it sustains right up until the subsequent note is played).

EXERCISE 32 *Beethoven – theme from 6th Symphony. The tie in bar seven means the F is held there for a total of five beats.*

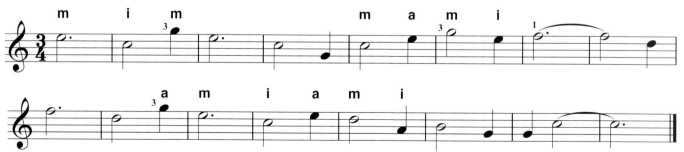

Here the tie is used to delay the next note in the upper part. This is done with a minim in bars three and four. **EXERCISE 33**

Anacrusis

The anacrusis, also known as an upbeat, is an extra beat coming just before the start of the first full bar. This note is on the last beat of an imaginary previous bar, and so to balance this the last bar of the piece has one less beat in it.

This can be seen in Exercise 34, which has only three beats in its last bar of ⁴⁄₄. Notice also that the last note has two stems (up and down): that's because this note is the end of both the upper and lower parts.

This whole piece is repeated - be sure to go straight to the anacrusis second-time around. Notice the tie in the first line: the G bass note is only played once, then left to ring until the D comes in. The third-string (G) is used as a bass string in bar one and six and played with **p**. **EXERCISE 34**

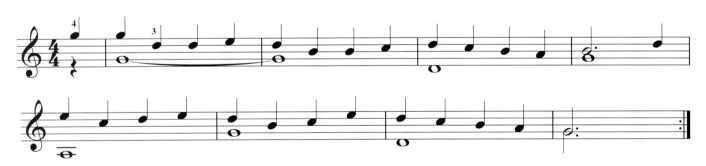

PLAY CLASSICAL GUITAR

SECTION ONE
PLAY CLASSICAL GUITAR

EXERCISE 35 *Minor waltz: a waltz, of course, means 3/4 time. Note the tie in the second to last bar – the C is held until the final D.*

EXERCISE 36 *This one works best if it's played quite quickly with a very steady pulse – but it should be learnt slowly at first, taking special care with the right-hand fingering.*

PLAY CLASSICAL GUITAR
SECTION TWO

Quavers

Sharps

Dotted rhythms

Key signatures

Intervals

The notes E & B

Counterpoint

Dynamics

Flats

Enharmonic equivalents

SECTION TWO
PLAY CLASSICAL GUITAR

Quavers (eighth-notes)

The quaver, or eighth-note, lasts half as long as a crotchet. So there are two quavers in a crotchet, four in a minim and eight in a semibreve. A quaver looks much like a crotchet except it has a tail at the end of the stem (♪ or ♩). When two or more quavers appear together they're connected by the tail – as in Exercise 37. Quavers are counted by saying "and" between each beat number. The quaver rest is 𝄾

EXERCISE 37 *Try to keep a steady crotchet pulse - don't let the quavers speed it up.*

1 & 2 & 3 & 4 &   1 & 2 & 3 & 4 &

EXERCISE 38 *'London's Burning' is a "round" and can be played with another guitar or other instrument: when the first player reaches beat three of bar two (the quaver D) the second player should start at the beginning. A third player can enter when player two has reached beat three, bar two, etc.*

EXERCISE 39 *Note the dotted minim rest in the second full bar - in this case it's functioning like a tie from the previous bass note, which should be left to ring for all three beats in this bar rather than stopped dead.*

Sharp sign:

When the sharp sign appears before a note on the stave the note is raised by a semitone (one fret). A semitone is the smallest standard interval in Western music (interval theory is dealt with in more detail later). In Exercise 40, F is raised to F-sharp at fret two, string one, and is played with finger 2. The sharp sign used this way is effective for a whole bar and is cancelled by the bar line.

SECTION TWO
PLAY CLASSICAL GUITAR

Don't speed up when playing the quavers in bar three – keep a regular beat. **EXERCISE 40**

The natural sign ♮ is used to cancel out a sharp used in the same bar, returning the note to its original pitch. When sharp, flat or natural symbols are used next to the note like this they are called "accidentals". **EXERCISE 41**

There are two new sharps here: C-sharp in bar one and D-sharp in bar four of line two. They will present no problem if you follow the exact fingering. **EXERCISE 42**

PLAY CLASSICAL GUITAR

SECTION TWO
PLAY CLASSICAL GUITAR

2/4 Time

The time signature of 2/4 indicates that there are two crotchets (quarter-beats) per bar. This is normally used for faster music than 4/4, and is often used with quavers.

EXERCISE 43 *'Pease Pudding Hot' (nursery rhyme): return to start immediately at end.*

The note A

Introducing the use of finger 4. As with the other three left-hand fingers, keep the fourth finger curved, bending the top joint as it comes down towards the string – otherwise you can lose strength and control. Bring it down gently, especially at first, to minimise wear and tear on this weakest digit. Don't try to stretch to reach this note either – move the hand temporarily out of position to hold it down. Now we have played three A notes (including the open fifth string) – spanning two full octaves in this key. Note the pattern your fingers make when you play octave notes, and how this pattern repeats, and where it changes, around the fingerboard.

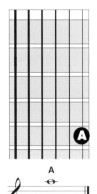

EXERCISE 44 *Rossini – 'William Tell Overture'. This piece has the latest, higher A at bar six, line two. To reach this note the left hand has to move out of position up to the fifth fret.*

Dotted rhythm

As explained at Exercise 18, adding a dot to a note increases its length by half. When a dotted note is used together with a note of the same value as the dot, the result is called a dotted rhythm. (For example, in bar one of Exercise 45 there's a dotted crotchet immediately followed by a quaver.) The desired effect is to create a rhythmic lilt in the music.

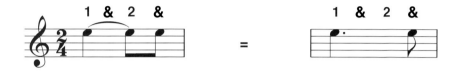

It is important to count when learning dotted rhythms so the dotted note is exactly the right length.

EXERCISE 45

*Again, the rest in bars four, six and eight means you keep the previous bass note ringing. The open G in bar one, line three is played with **p**.*

EXERCISE 46

SECTION TWO
PLAY CLASSICAL GUITAR

Key signatures

When particular notes are always sharp in a piece of music, this is indicated by sharps at the beginning of each line, and it affects all the notes of that pitch throughout the whole work. When the symbols are written at the beginning of each line like this it's called a key signature. A key is a hierarchy of chords and notes, the main one of which is called a tonic or key note. In Exercise 47 the key is G, which has a signature of one sharp (F-sharp). This key signature is shared by its relative minor - in this case E minor, which is the key used in Exercise 48. (There's more on key signatures on p67.)

EXERCISE 47 *The first couple of F-sharps are marked above the notes as a reminder – after that you must remember to sharpen any other Fs in this key.*

EXERCISE 48 *Here the sharpened Fs are in bar two... Watch out for the D-sharp accidental in the second bar of line two.*

Notes E and F on the fourth string

SECTION TWO
PLAY CLASSICAL GUITAR

These two neighbouring notes on the D-string – played with fingers 2 and 3 respectively – are plucked with the right-hand thumb (**p**). They're the first left-hand bass notes we've seen so far, but it's the kind of combination that often crops up in a bass part. Practise going from E to F and back as fluidly and evenly as possible. When playing Exercise 49, be especially aware of the points where you change from a fretted note to an open string, and listen for any difference in tone – this can be particularly marked when moving from a wound to an unwound string. Practise these changes till the alteration in sound quality is minimal.

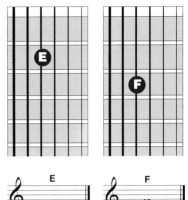

All notes played with the thumb – even the third-string A in line one.   **EXERCISE 49**

EXERCISE 50 *The word "rall" near the end here is short for rallentando, which means "slowing down". This is to be done gradually throughout the section indicated by the dotted line.*

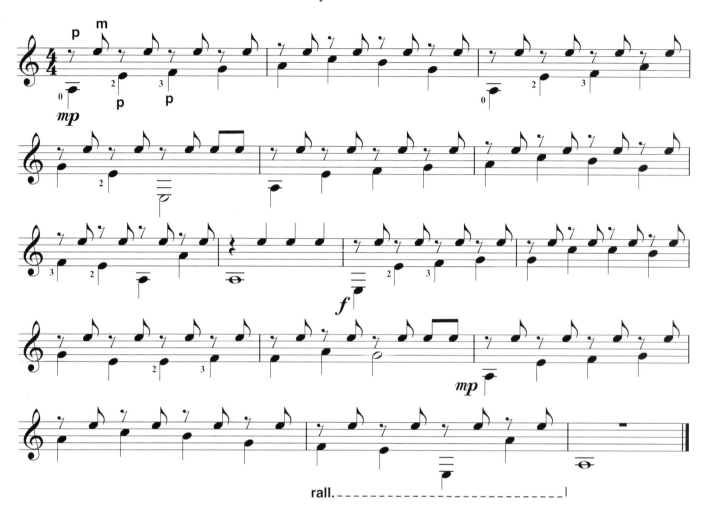

Intervals

SECTION TWO
PLAY CLASSICAL GUITAR

An interval is the "vertical" distance between two notes. Intervals can be played simultaneously (to build chords or harmony) or consecutively (to create melody). Although there are 12 intervals in all, at this point we'll only deal with three: 3rds, 4ths and 5ths. The size (or number) of an interval is calculated by counting upwards from the lower note, which is itself counted as 1. For example, the interval between G and B is a third (G, A, B).

*Keep fingers **m** and **i** stuck together when you play this one.* **EXERCISE 51**

*In the last bar here, three notes are played simultaneously, making a chord. This is played in a similar way to using **p** and **m** together. Here, **m** and **i** do the top parts and **p** does the bass. Remember to keep the fingers back and the thumb forward so there's room to manoeuvre.* **EXERCISE 52**

The second line here uses the same notes as the first, but splits the intervals. **EXERCISE 53**

SECTION TWO
PLAY CLASSICAL GUITAR

Notes B and C

Similar to the combination of E and F on the D-string (page 37), this time one string lower on the fifth string, the A. Again, these would appear in a bass part played with the thumb. In the next exercise, see how consistently you can move from one note to the next without any unwanted ringing of open strings. (Smooth playing technique, or "legato", will be covered in more detail later in the book.) Exercise 54 makes use of all the left-hand bass notes – including open-strings – that we've learnt so far on the fourth and fifth strings.

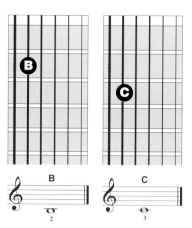

EXERCISE 54 *An alternative version of Exercise 49, but a fourth lower, on the A-string.*

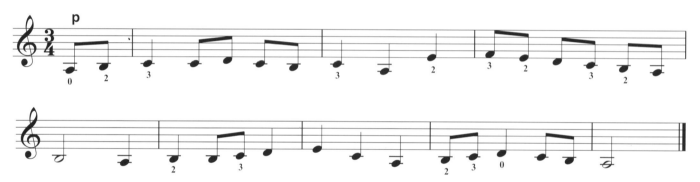

Counterpoint

So far all the two-part music in the book has had one relatively static voice (a simple bass part, perhaps) and another more animated (either the upper voice melody or moving bass). In the second half of Exercise 55, both parts are quite active and have a harmonic function – this is known as counterpoint. Music with two or more active voices is called "contrapuntal" ("using counterpoint").

SECTION TWO
PLAY CLASSICAL GUITAR

The word "rit" near the end here is short for ritardo, meaning "delayed" or "held back". In contrast to rallentando, where the music is simply slowed down, ritardo is used to give a sense of lingering on the notes before the end, to heighten the expectation of the piece's conclusion.

EXERCISE 55

SECTION TWO
PLAY CLASSICAL GUITAR

Dynamics

Dynamics are the varying levels and changes of volume in a piece of music. This is indicated for all instruments by the letters *p*, *f* and *m*, which are abbreviations of the Italian words:

piano – soft or quiet
forte – strong or loud
mezzo – medium

The letters are often found in combinations, such as *mp* (mezzo piano) or *mf* (mezzo forte). More extreme volumes are indicated by the doubling, tripling or more of the letters for example: *ff* – fortissimo (very loud), *fff* – molto fortissimo (extremely loud), *ppp* – molto pianissimo (extremely quiet).

Gradual changes of volume are indicated using special line symbols, nicknamed "hairpins" (see below). These affect the entire section of music they're positioned under.
Dynamics are always written under the stave, except on vocal music where they would interfere with printed words.

    < = crescendo (getting louder).

    > = diminuendo (getting quieter).

EXERCISE 56 *A very simple exercise musically – the idea is to work on the dynamics.*

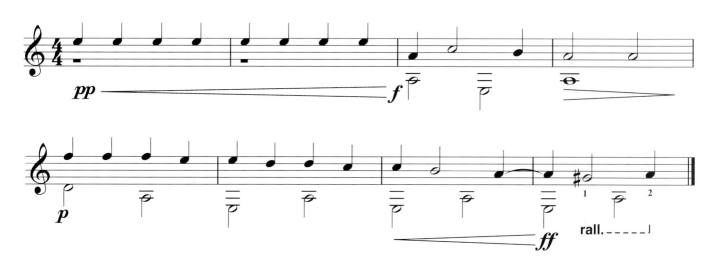

This starts loud, gets quiet at bar two, line two, then gets louder again (and slows down) towards the end. Watch out for the arpeggios changing direction at various points.

EXERCISE 57

EXERCISE 58 *Polish folk song: in bars seven and eight the symbol > can be seen above some notes. This is an accent that tells the performer to play these particular notes much louder than the others.*

Notes F and G on the sixth string

SECTION TWO
PLAY CLASSICAL GUITAR

As there are two E-strings on a guitar (first and sixth strings), obviously all the notes on the sixth string are the same as those we looked at on the first, just two octaves lower. So F is at fret I, played with finger 1, and G is at fret III, played with finger 3.

Exercise 59 is to be played apoyando (rest stroke) with **p** throughout, apart from the final chord where, because of the upper notes, tirando is much easier. The slight volume loss here is made up for by the extra notes.

The symbol 𝄐 over the last beat of the last bar is a "fermata" or pause – this means you should hold this chord for longer than its rhythmic value.

This starts with an upbeat, but the accent moves in each bar (check on CD).   **EXERCISE 59**

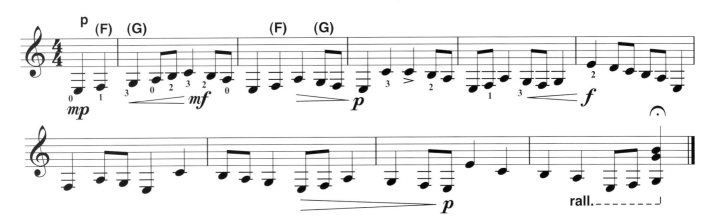

This whole piece is repeated once. The numbers above the last two bars indicate that, on the first play-through, the bar marked 1 is to be played here, which leads back to the start. When repeating the piece this bar is left out and the final bar, marked 2, is played in its place. These are known as first and second time bars.   **EXERCISE 60**

PLAY CLASSICAL GUITAR
45

SECTION TWO
PLAY CLASSICAL GUITAR

6/8 Time

This time signature is also known as compound-duple time – this just means the bar has two halves, each of which has three beats. As with all time signatures, the top number refers to the amount of beats per bar (six in this case) and the lower number indicates the unit (a quaver or eighth-note here). 6/8 has a particular feel to it, stemming from the two groups of three in each bar, found elsewhere only in the rarer time signatures of 6/16 and 6/4.

EXERCISE 61 *Finger 3 is used for the A in bar five to make it easier for finger 2 to get to the E in bar six.*

Here we have five previously unused sharps in the bass part: F-sharp in bar one, C-sharp in bar three, D-sharp in bar six, F-sharp on the fourth string in bar one of line two, and A-sharp in bar three of line two. Follow the given fingering exactly and these accidentals will present no problem.

EXERCISE 62

SECTION TWO
PLAY CLASSICAL GUITAR

Semiquavers (16th-notes)

The semiquaver, or 16th-note ♪ looks like a quaver, with two tails on the stem, and has half the rhythmic value (ie it's twice as fast as a quaver). So there are two semiquavers per quaver, and four in a crotchet. As with quavers, semiquavers connect when they appear in a group (the tails straighten out and link up), as in bar three in Exercise 63 below. They can also connect to quavers, as in bar four. The semiquaver rest is 𝄾

EXERCISE 63 *This helps show the relationship between crotchets, quavers and semiquavers.*

EXERCISE 64 *'Mechanical Ballet' - plenty of semiquavers, rests, ties and dynamics*

EXERCISE 65

There is a dotted rhythm here made up of a quaver and a semiquaver. This functions in exactly the same way as the previously covered dotted rhythm of crotchet and quaver. The dotted quaver is worth three semiquavers which, together with the semiquaver, completes the crotchet unit. When practising this piece it's best to learn the top part first, then add the bass part.

EXERCISE 66

*This exercise uses a typical right-hand pattern for the guitar: the tune is in the bass, and both the harmony and rhythm are provided by the arpeggio of **p**, **i** and **m**. This piece will sound best when played quite fast. First, practise the right-hand arpeggio pattern by itself (**p**, **i** and **m**). Then learn the bass tune (all played with **p**) without the arpeggio notes. And finally put the two together. This way the piece can be learned very accurately and quickly. When you feel comfortable, try to play it without the music – as mentioned before, this will allow you to watch your left-hand movements, and also build a stronger identification with the piece.*

Flat sign: ♭

SECTION TWO
PLAY CLASSICAL GUITAR

Flats operate in a similar way to sharps except they lower the note by a semitone rather than raise it.

Flats are used both as accidentals and in key signatures, but in the latter they're never mixed with sharps – key signatures have either flats or sharps but never both.

You can see from the diagram on the next page that flat notes co-exist with sharps at certain places on the guitar fingerboard – for instance, B-flat = A-sharp, and F-sharp = G-flat. This is known as "enharmony" – these notes are enharmonic equivalents: the particular note name used at any one time will depend on which scale or key is being employed, and whether the music is rising or falling.

At bar six, finger 4 must slide on the string from the A to the A-flat. **EXERCISE 67**

Lots of flat accidentals here, and the occasional sharp to watch for. Stick to the given fingering throughout; and let the G ring on in bar three line two, so it creates a harmony with the E-flat starting the next bar. **EXERCISE 68**

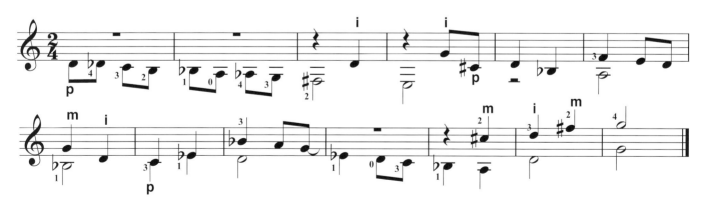

PLAY CLASSICAL GUITAR

SECTION TWO
PLAY CLASSICAL GUITAR

The first two lines below show the same notes as lines three and four, but using flats instead of sharps. These are enharmonic equivalents. (Try playing both examples – they sound exactly the same.)

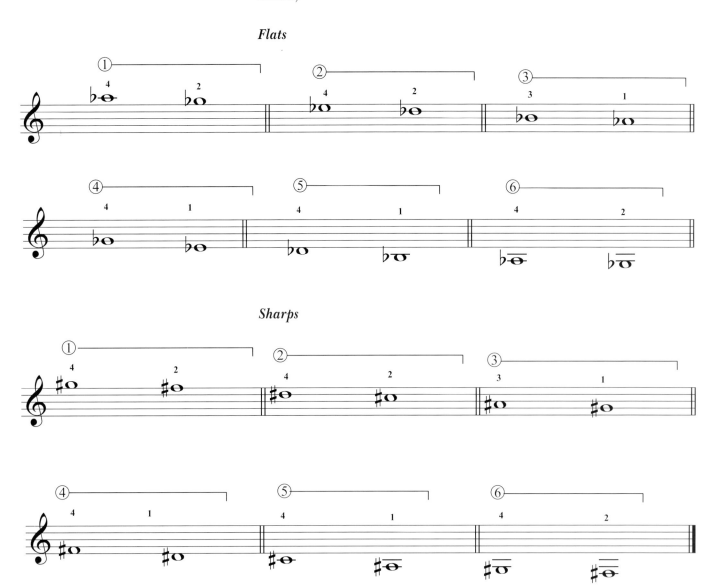

Time for a familiar piece that uses many of the techniques we've looked at so far. 'Greensleeves' was composed during the reign of Henry VIII (and is even sometimes attributed to him) – it's typical of the lute style of Renaissance England. The work is in three sections, marked with a boxed A, B and AA – at AA the first theme returns, this time with a more active bass part.

EXERCISE 70

In Exercise 70, titled 'Little Fantasia', there are several places where two notes are held simultaneously with the left hand (for instance in bars four, five and six). Following the written fingering is essential here, but these sections should also be practised separately from the rest of the piece until they feel comfortable. It's a good idea to practise the left-hand movements alone, especially when there's a jump from one set of two notes to another (as from the E and G-sharp to the F and A in the first bar of line two). There's a new sharp in bar three of line three: G-sharp on string six at the fourth fret.

PLAY CLASSICAL GUITAR
SECTION THREE

Memorisation

Tempo

Crescendo & diminuendo

Interval qualities

Legato

Second position (II)

Order of sharps & flats

Irrational rhythms

Arpeggios – part two

Melody within arpeggio

Damping

Half-barre

SECTION THREE
PLAY CLASSICAL GUITAR

Memorisation

When you're still at the stage of learning to play the guitar, each new piece you approach can throw up a lot of things to deal with at once – such as fingering, hand position and reading the score.

Ideally pieces should always be played from memory, as this allows you to concentrate on these other factors. Even the simple practicality of not having to look at the printed score makes the enormous difference of letting you watch the left hand closely and so guide its movement more easily.

There are three main types of memory at work in musical performance. They are:

- **Audio** – how the music sounds, for example the contour of a theme or type of rhythm.
- **Tactile** – the memory of shapes and patterns made by the hands, which to a large extent is retained in the hands themselves. This is especially evident in the left hand where the shapes are more static.
- **Visual** – this applies both to the remembered image of the score and also to the above-mentioned shapes and movement patterns of the left hand.

There is a degree of deliberate choice involved in using the different types of memory, but the ideal combination of all three is apportioned naturally. The way a piece is memorised greatly affects how quickly it is mastered, and in turn directly affects the development of your playing.

When learning a new work it is important to choose a piece that's at an appropriate ability level. For beginners this is easily done just by following the order of the exercises in this book.

Players who may already be accomplished guitarists but not up to speed with written music would be best learning pieces within reasonable technical reach but of sufficient complexity and interest to warrant memorisation. This applies especially to guitarists who play chord-based styles of music such as rock or jazz – they may find the pieces towards the end of this section most suitable.

The first step is to try playing the entire piece through once. If this proves too difficult, or takes so long that no overall view is gained, then try playing through just the first four bars until they become familiar. Do this for the rest of the piece until all of it has been played, even if only in parts.

The next step is to learn to play the entire work from beginning to end without too many mistakes. When you've achieved this, which may take a few days, try playing without the score, even if you still have to slow down at the more difficult parts, or hit the occasional wrong note.

At first attempt you might find you have a complete blank after the opening few notes. This is not unusual and shouldn't put you off trying to memorise the piece. Just put the guitar down and study the score on its own to find where you went wrong, and what notes come next.

Say, for example, the first three notes of a piece are A, B, C and the next are B, B, A – but you can only remember the first two and stick at the C. The thing to do is to keep looking at the score until that following B, B, A is fixed in your mind.

This next bit is the most important. When you go back to the guitar (putting away the score) you must start from the beginning of the piece and play right through the problematic section.

This technique helps you memorise pieces quickly, and fixes the work in your mind for longer.

Tempo

As well as the actual notes and rhythms, there are many other nuances that composers may want to convey to performers to help put their musical intentions across accurately. An example of this is the notation of dynamics and the use of "rit" and "rall" covered earlier. But the general speed at which a piece is to be played (its "tempo") and an indication of its overall character are usually shown on the stave by the use of particular Italian words.

The most regularly used are:

Presto – quick
Allegro – lively or merry
Vivace – vivacious, full of life
Andante – moving along, walking pace
Moderato – moderate, similar to andante
Largo – broad, slow, dignified
Adagio – at ease, slow (less slow than largo)
Lento – slow
Grave – slow and solemn

Variations of the above work either as superlatives or more subtle versions, such as:

Adagissimo – extremely slow
Prestissimo – very quick
Allegretto – pretty lively but less so than allegro
Larghetto – still slow, but not as slow as largo

Since the invention of the metronome (by Maelzel, during Beethoven's era), tempo is often shown by an exact figure giving the number of beats per minute.

For example ♩ = 60 (60 crotchets per minute) would be a tempo of a beat per second. This type of tempo indication is called a metronome mark, and is sometimes written MM ♩ = 60. The MM is an abbreviation of Maelzel's Metronome.

Dynamics – part two

In addition to the hairpin dynamic markings discussed in Section Two, verbal instructions (again in Italian) are also often used: for example, "cresc....." or "dim....." (short for crescendo and diminuendo, "getting louder" or "getting quieter"), with the dotted line indicating where and for how long the dynamic change is to occur.

The metronome marking given for this piece is a final goal – initially the work must be learned considerably slower so the left hand has ample time to assimilate the movements properly, and perform them very smoothly.

EXERCISE 71

EXERCISE 72 *This exercise has a flat key signature (D minor) which has one flat (B-flat). The piece has three parts, or voices, and generally the top two move together in parallel. At bar one in line two, the middle voice separates from the top one and has movement of its own. This also happens in the top voice at bar three, line two, and again later in the piece. The four-note chords at bars one and two of line six are played just like the right-hand chord exercise at the start of Section One – all the notes must sound together.*

Intervals – part two

In Exercise 72 there was a new interval – a 6th between B-flat and G at bar four. Every interval, as well as having a number, has what is known as a "quality": this can be diminished, minor, major, perfect or augmented. In simple terms, the quality of the interval determines how large it is exactly, and how it relates to other intervals: for instance a major 3rd is a semitone larger than a minor 3rd.

The intervals are connected to the key in which they're found: a minor key such as D minor (as used in Exercise 72) has a minor 3rd (three semitones) from its tonic note D to its 3rd, F; a major key such as C (Exercise 71) has a major 3rd (four semitones) from its tonic note C to its 3rd, E.

Intervals can also be inverted (turned upside down): the resulting interval will be the numerical difference between the original interval and the number 9, and the "quality" will also reverse. For example, the minor 3rd 'G to B-flat' (Example 1) when inverted will become the major 6th 'B-flat to G' (Example 2).

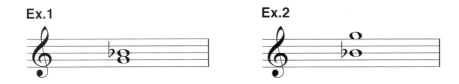

Below are all 12 intervals (shown in the key of C to avoid sharps and flats). There's also another type of interval known as a "compound interval". This is simply the result of a normal interval added to the octave (with the octave note counting as one) – so, for example, a major 10th is simply a major 3rd plus an octave.

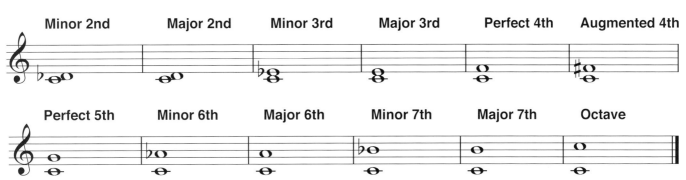

SECTION THREE
PLAY CLASSICAL GUITAR

Legato

Notes played on the guitar have a definite attack with a rather rapid decay of the sound. As a result, if you want to make the music flow smoothly, it's necessary to connect one note to the next so there's no break in the sound. Practise the examples below.

Going from an open string to a fretted note, as in Example 1, you need to be careful – when reaching over the first string to play the C with finger 1, you mustn't touch the top E and stop it sounding.

When going from a fretted note to a different open string, as in Example 2, it's important not to touch the open-string B with finger 2, but also not to remove the A until after the B is sounding.

When changing from a fretted note to the same open string, as in Example 3, the first note, D, must stay on and be sounding until the right-hand finger is already on the string to play the second note, the open B. The D is only released at the last moment.

When the situation is reversed, going from an open string to a fretted note, as in Example 4, the finger that plays the fretted note (D in this case) should not be placed on the string too early. Ideally it should arrive on the string at exactly the same time as the right-hand finger, so by the time the right-hand finger releases the string, the fretting finger is already holding the note down.

Going from one fretted note to another is done in the same way. In Example 5, the C must be held until the D is already being played by the right hand.

It's the same in the other direction. When going from D to C, the D must be held on by finger 3 until the C is held down and the right-hand finger is on the string, just about to release it and make it sound.

Although the movements may seem a bit complex at first, they all work on the same basic principle of keeping the string sounding at all times.

The five examples on the left-hand page should all be practised separately and then played together as Exercise 73.

SECTION THREE
PLAY CLASSICAL GUITAR

EXERCISE 73

Some new instances of legato playing arise here, such as crossing the strings from one fretted note to another – C to A, going from bar one to bar two.

EXERCISE 74

This brings in fingers 2 and 4. Play legato throughout – for example, with the first two notes, make sure finger 4 stays on till the C plays; in bar three, hold the top F over the G; hold the G-sharp right through bar four.

From here on all pieces should be played legato – it's essential this becomes a standard part of the left-hand technique. Although you may find this distracts you from other new techniques you encounter, remember that at this stage you needn't do everything at once.

For example if you are faced with a demanding exercise containing some new notes, learn those first; then when things become more familiar the piece can be refined using legato and paying attention to tone quality and tempo.

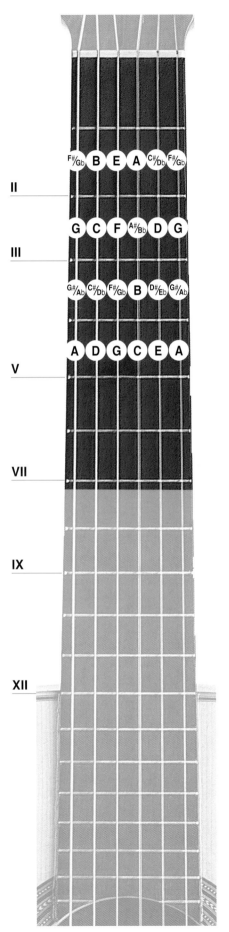

Second position (II)

The second position is when the first finger is used to play notes at fret two (such as A, C-sharp and F-sharp). With the hand a fret higher up the fingerboard, finger two now plays the notes at fret three, finger 3 plays those at fret four, and finger 4 those at fret five.

Although finger 4 has been used previously to play the high A at fret five on the first string, this involved a small stretch and a momentary move out of first position and is advisable only for the occasional note. When playing in second position this A and all the other notes at the fifth fret are easily within reach.

Position is indicated in guitar notation by Roman numerals, so second position is written as II, third as III and so on. The fact that the fifth fret is used for tuning purposes (as we saw in Section One) will help when it comes to memorising the notes at this fret – other than the C on the 3rd string, they're the same as the adjacent, higher open string.

Playing in second position is particularly useful for the key of D major, which has two sharps (F-sharp and C-sharp), as well as for reaching the high A at fret five, which is an interval of a perfect 5th away from the tonic note D, and so plays a very important role.

In music using the key system, the note that is a 5th away from the tonic is called the "dominant". This is at the pivotal mid-point of a scale, about as far as it is possible to move from the tonic before starting to come back "home" to the octave note. As such it functions crucially as a contrasting but complementary note to the key or tonic.

Fingerboard showing notes at second position.

This exercise is in D major (two sharps: F-sharp and C-sharp) and stays in second position throughout.

EXERCISE 75

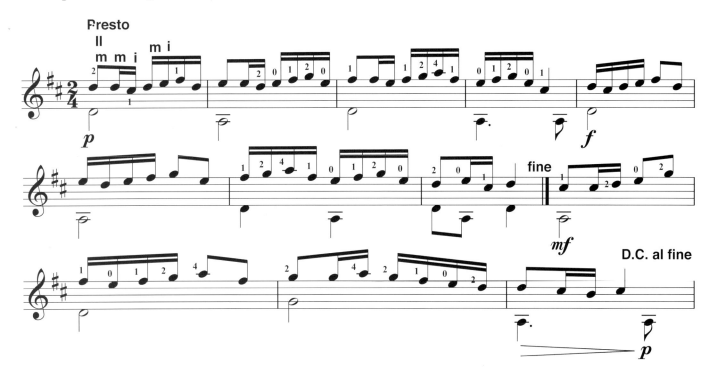

This piece is also in D major, and moves from position II to position I at bar four and then back again to position II at bar five. At bars two and three in line three make sure you hold on the B bass note with finger 1 while playing the moving upper part with fingers 3 and 2.

EXERCISE 76

Order of sharps & flats

When indicating a key signature with one or more sharps, the order is always the same on the stave:

(from left to right) F♯, C♯, G♯, D♯, A♯, E♯, B♯.

A simple way of remembering the order of sharps is by using the mnemonic: Father Charles Goes Down And Eats Breakfast.

The order of flats is simply the reverse of the sharps:

B♭, E♭, A♭, D♭, G♭, C♭, F♭ (or even: By Eating All Day Greedy Charles Fattens).

You can use the same mnemonics to help work out the key of a piece from the number of sharps and flats at the start, although here the letter cycle starts on C (as that's the key with no sharps or flats). In other words:

Number of sharps: 0 1 2 3 4 5 6
Key: C G D A E B F

Number of flats: 0 1 2 3 4 5 6
Key: C F B♭ E♭ A♭ D♭ G♭

So the key with five sharps (B) is shown at the start of the stave as F♯, C♯, G♯, D♯, A♯. The key of E (four sharps) is written: F♯, C♯, G♯, D♯. The key of F (one flat) has B♭ at the start. And E♭ (three flats) is shown as B♭, E♭, A♭.

The main theme of 'Spring' from The Four Seasons by Vivaldi (1676 – 1741). It's in the key of A (meaning A major – when not otherwise specified a key is always major). This key has three sharps to watch out for: F-sharp, C-sharp and G-sharp. The piece takes off nicely if played fast and steady; and remember not to pause at the end of line one – it's straight back to the start. Lines two and three repeat too.

EXERCISE 77

SECTION THREE
PLAY CLASSICAL GUITAR

Irrational rhythms

Although the terminology can be rather daunting, these rhythms have a simple concept. An irrational, or "irregular", rhythm (also known as "tuplets") is where more beats are put into a bar than is allowed by the time signature. This is possible by speeding the beats up by a certain ratio, indicated by a number written over (or under) the relevant group of notes.

The most common irrational rhythm is a triplet, which has a ratio of 3:2 – a crotchet triplet has three crotchets played in the time it normally takes to play two (as in Example 1 below).

This can also be done with other note values, such as a quaver (see Example 2).

Irrational rhythms can be made up of any ratio – another common one is the sextuplet (6:4 – see Example 3).

Less common in older music but often found in Art music of the mid-to-late 20th century are the quintuplet (5:4 – Example 4) and septuplet (7:4 – Example 5).

EXAMPLE 1

EXAMPLE 2

EXAMPLE 3

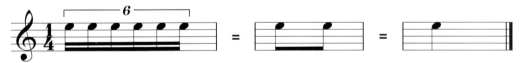

EXAMPLE 4

EXAMPLE 5

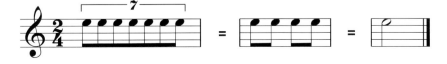

The quintuplet and septuplet are usually counted by dividing them into two parts – for example a quintuplet can be a three and a two, or vice versa, and a septuplet can be counted as four and a three, or vice versa.

SECTION THREE
PLAY CLASSICAL GUITAR

EXERCISE 78

This exercise uses triplets throughout (though notice that the triplets are only actually written in for the first bar or so, to avoid cluttering up the score too much). It's in the key of A and moves position a number of times, as shown. You should work up to the tempo indication – practise it quite slowly until both hands feel confident with the different kinds of movement.

Molto Rall.

SECTION THREE
PLAY CLASSICAL GUITAR

Arpeggios – part two

In the next exercise there are places where the left hand holds down three notes simultaneously, making full chords. By the time you've reached this stage in the book your left hand will have gained enough strength to do this, but be sure to make smooth and quick changes between chords, with each finger taking the shortest route from one position to another, so the tempo of the music doesn't drop. As with the right hand, the left-hand chord changes should be practised on their own.

EXERCISE 79

*This is largely a right-hand exercise in full arpeggio. The right-hand pattern should be practised separately, making sure the hand does not move while playing, and that the tone and volume are consistent across the strings. On beats two and three of bar four, the right-hand pattern changes strings so the fingers are now playing strings four, three and two. The final chord is an E minor, to be played with the thumb strumming across the strings – as indicated by the wavy line just before the chord. The arrow at the top of this line shows the movement should be upwards in pitch (which means the thumb going **down** the strings). The highest (last) note of this chord, the E, should land on the beat, so the note "spread" must begin slightly before.*

SECTION THREE
PLAY CLASSICAL GUITAR

Melody within arpeggio

This technique is very characteristic of the guitar and is a practical and effective way of providing a combination of melody, rhythm and harmony – three fundamental aspects of music.

EXERCISE 80

As in Exercises 66 and 79, the arpeggio here provides both harmony and rhythm, but in this piece the melody is in the top part, indicated by notes with the stems pointing upwards. These notes are to be played slightly louder than the rest – best achieved by keeping the arpeggio part (the semiquavers) **pp** *in volume. As in Exercise 79, the right hand here should be practised separately, with the* **a** *finger slightly accenting the notes on the top string. The symbol ⊕ at the end of bar three means that when you reach this point (after the repeat) you jump from the first sign to the second one and immediately play the final bar as an ending to the whole piece.*

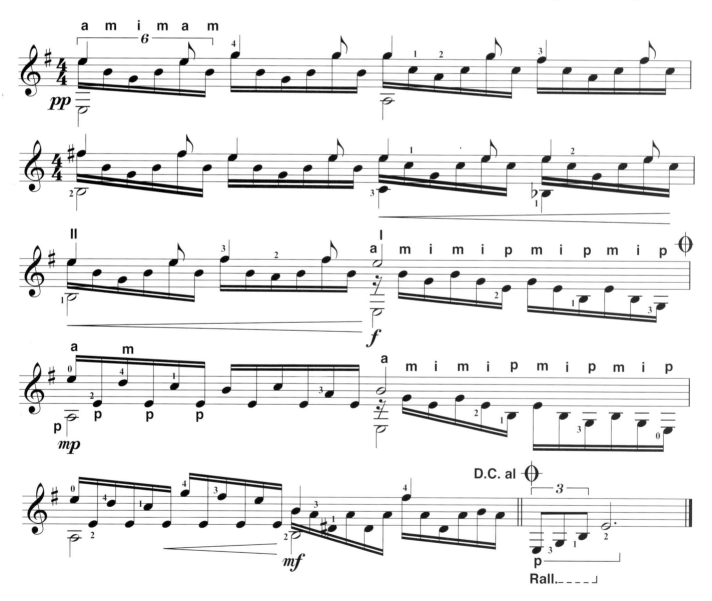

Damping

Sometimes the sustain of the bass notes on the guitar is too long for certain moments in a piece, and can give a rather untidy and harmonically confusing impression if left to ring. This can be solved by damping the unwanted string with the right-hand thumb.

When going from a high string to a lower one – such as from A to the low E (as in Example 1, below) – a simple apoyando will stop the A ringing.

When going the opposite way (as in Example 2, below), the E can be stopped by bending the first joint on the right-hand thumb slightly while playing the A. The top of the thumb, behind the nail, should make contact with the E-string exactly when the A is played (but not before), making a smooth transition from E to A while at the same time preventing the E from covering the sound of the A. (See photographs on next page too.)

This technique could be put to good use in Exercise 79, just before the penultimate bar, going from the E in the previous bar to the first of the last three chords.

SECTION THREE
PLAY CLASSICAL GUITAR

These two photographs show the subtle shape change made by the thumb in order to "damp" the lower string and to stop it sounding.

Half-barre

The half-barre is a way of holding down more than one string at a time with only one finger. It is especially useful when several notes on the same fret are required (as in the example notated below).

The symbol used in notation for a half-barre is the fraction "½" next to a capital letter C, with the position number where the half-barre is to be placed. The half-barre is normally held with finger 1, and covers between two and four strings

A common place for the half-barre is at the second position (II), where the notes of F-sharp, C-sharp and A might be held down on strings one, two and three (as mentioned before these are important notes in the key of D). But it can be used anywhere on the neck, and we'll see it again later in the book when we look at the higher positions.

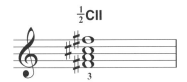

The photograph of the half-barre above shows the position of the thumb (opposite finger 2) and which part of finger 1 is used to hold down the strings. In the photo on the left note that the finger making the half-barre is exactly parallel to the fret, but not so close as to damp the sounding strings.

EXERCISE 81

'Morning Chant' – the half-barre is used at the second fret for the first three bars to allow the A and F-sharp to ring over the tune and create background harmony. Although there are two notes of A at the start of the first bar this is only notational, to show that the initial quaver A has a secondary function, lasting as a dotted minim underneath the quaver movement in the upper part. The metronome marking shows the tempo of a dotted crotchet beat (three quavers).

PLAY CLASSICAL GUITAR
SECTION FOUR

Ligado

Chords

Third position (III)

Octave shapes

Full-barre

Ligado – part two

Fifth position (V)

Ornaments

SECTION FOUR
PLAY CLASSICAL GUITAR

Ligado

The ligado, or slur, is denoted by a curved line between two notes of different pitch. It's similar to a tie, except that's only used between notes of the same pitch, as we saw in Section One.

A ligado is used for making particularly smooth or quick left-hand changes between notes (beyond what can be comfortably achieved when plucking each note individually with the right hand).

You can make a ligado with any of the left-hand fingers – it usually depends which position you're playing in and which note is to be slurred to or from.

There are two types of ligado: going up and going down – ie slurring *to* a note or *from* a note. Slurring up to a note is easier, so we'll start with that. In Example 1, below, there is a slur from G to A. The G is played with the right hand and the A is played with the left hand, sounded by coming down onto the note rapidly with the fingertip.

Examples 2 and 3 work on the same principle but are played with fingers 1 and 3 respectively. Example 4 is different in that the first note, C, is also a fretted note. In this case you must use this note as if it were an open string and keep it on when slurring onto the second note, the D.

The main points to remember in playing ligado are to bring the left-hand finger down exactly at the moment the note is to sound, because this finger is actually "playing" the note. This is slightly later than if you were plucking the note, where the left-hand finger would come down earlier to be ready for the right hand to play/pluck the string.

It's also very important that the finger comes down firmly so a percussive strike is made on the string, producing enough volume to match a plucked note.

This exercise makes use of ligado with various fingers. The most difficult is at bar two line two, between fingers 2 and 4. It's important the rhythm is not affected by the use of the slurs - the slurred quavers must still arrive at the right moment, not too early.

EXERCISE 82

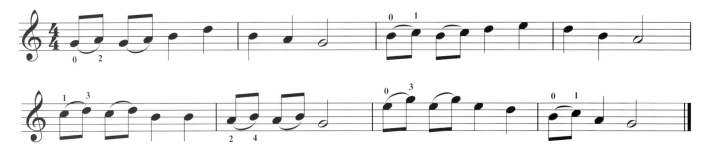

Chords

The guitar is a harmonic instrument – which means, like a piano or harp, it's capable of harmony as well as melody. Harmony is the movement of chords or implied chords in relation to a theme or line of music played simultaneously. The use of harmony of some kind is common to most music, though the notes and types of chord obey different rules according to the period and style of the music.

Most of the exercises in this book are written using the "Tonal System" of harmony, which was the dominant force in Art music from the Renaissance up until the first decades of the 20th century when other forms of harmonic and compositional techniques came into use – largely because the combinations available within the existing tonal system began to be overused. (There's more about these newer systems in Section Five.)

The tonal system is still the most familiar musical language, thanks to the enduring nature of a lot of older classical music, and also its continued use in popular music. Although we don't have space to go into detail in this book, there is a growing repertoire for the guitar using newer systems, and it's important to become familiar with them whenever you can.

Tonality is based on the idea of a particular chord, known as the Tonic (abbreviated as the Roman numeral I), used as a starting point from which the music travels and to which it returns. In opposition to the tonic there is a chord called the dominant (V), which is a perfect 5th higher (or perfect 4th lower).

The other main chord used in tonality is the subdominant (IV) which is a perfect 4th higher than the tonic (or perfect 5th lower, and a tone lower than the dominant).

The tension and release that gives music its sense of movement is created by the pull between these chords (known as the primary chords) via other secondary chords.

SECTION FOUR
PLAY CLASSICAL GUITAR

The basis of each chord is a "triad", which is made up of three notes. Triads can be major, minor, diminished and augmented, rather like intervals. A triad has two intervals: a third (major or minor depending on key) and a perfect 5th (both counted from the root).

Another way to put it is to say that a triad is made up of two thirds placed above each other. A major triad is a major 3rd with a minor 3rd above it. A minor triad is the reverse – a minor 3rd with a major 3rd above it.

Triads can have more notes added to them and still have the same function, as long as the extra notes are more of those already in the chord – this is called "doubling", and usually involves octaves above the constituent notes.

In the last example below, the C major triad has been expanded by doubling the C (the root note) and the E (the third) an octave higher (in this case making the top two notes of the chord).

Major Triad of C

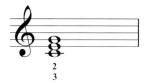

Minor Triad of C minor

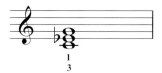

C Major

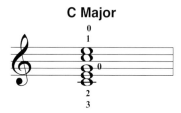

Chord diagrams

The main method of notation for guitar chords is the chord diagram. This is a very clear system which has the advantage of being understood by non-readers of standard music notation. It's basically a small map or picture of the fingerboard showing which string and which fret the fingers are to hold down. The strings with x above them are not to be played.

Below are diagrams for the three primary chords in two keys, E and C. The dominant chord in the key of E is a dominant 7th (B7) – again often used for changing key, and a familiar chord in guitar music in the key of E.

Also included are the two minor chords, E minor (Em) and A minor (Am). If Em and Am are substituted for E and A, you will have the primary chords for the key of E minor (B7, the dominant, stays major). The chord of A minor is known as the relative (submediant, VI) of C, and fits well in the progression C, Am, F and G.

SECTION FOUR
PLAY CLASSICAL GUITAR

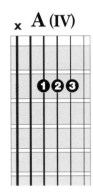

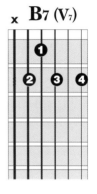

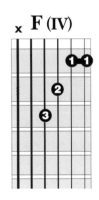

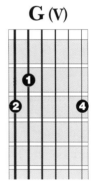

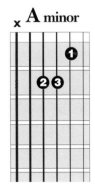

The first three chord diagrams show the primary chords for the key of E. The Roman numerals indicate tonic (I), subdominant (IV) and dominant (V). An x above a string means the string is not to be played.

The second set of three chords are the primary ones for the key of C. The chord of F requires two notes (F and C) to be held down with finger 1, using a small half-barre.

The final two minor chords are generally very useful and can be combined with the progressions above as follows: E minor and A minor can be substituted for E and A in the first progression, giving the primary chords in the key of E minor (Em and Am become I and V). Am can be inserted between C and F in the second progression, making C, Am, F, G, a four-chord pattern – in this case Am functions as VI, the submediant or relative minor.

SECTION FOUR
PLAY CLASSICAL GUITAR

Chords are best played either using the thumb, **p,** or with the back of the right-hand fingers, which is called "rasguedo" (in fact rasguedo is used to refer to all kinds of strumming, but specifically using the fingers).

The two methods sound very different: using **p** gives a rather warm and full sound, and is most appropriate when playing a chord as part of a classical piece, so there's not a sudden drop in the strength and type of tone (although pieces from the Baroque guitar repertoire use many types of strums and strumming patterns, including use of the back of the fingers).

The finger rasguedo uses the backs of the nails, and sounds thinner, less weighty, more percussive. It's also less controllable, unless you learn flamenco-type techniques, which are not within the scope of this book.

Using the thumb to play chords allows the exact speed of the movement across the strings to be controlled, so a slow, arpeggio-like motion can be played quite easily.

EXERCISE 83

*Theme from The Surprise Symphony by Haydn (1732-1809). There is one loud chord at the end – originally put in by the composer to stop audiences talking during the performance. The word "sempre" before the dynamic marking **pp** means "always", so the entire piece is played **pp** until a different dynamic is met. This happens at the chord marked **sfz**, short for sforzando, meaning forced – an indication to accent the chord heavily and suddenly (strummed very quickly with **p**). As there's no wavy line next to the chord, it is not to be spread.*

Third position (III)

Third position means finger 1 plays the notes at the third fret, finger 2 those at the fourth fret, and so on. This position allows finger 4 to reach the sixth fret, which brings into play the new note of high A-sharp/B-flat on the first string.

The other notes at the sixth fret are the same as those on the first fret on the next highest string. So the D-sharp/E-flat on string five, fret six is the same note as that found at string four, fret one.

A good way to help commit the fretboard to memory is to learn the order of the notes "vertically" across each fret as a distinct unit, as well as learning the positions "horizontally" up the neck. (Use the neck diagram on the fold-out page.)

It's useful to remember that the relationship of each note to every other note never changes. For example, D on string two is two frets away from C on the same string (frets three and one). It follows that D will also be two frets away from C on the third string – frets seven and five.

If you take a few minutes to look for these patterns on the instrument and repeat them up the fingerboard, the higher positions will lose some of their seemingly mysterious quality.

Octave shapes

Another way to get to know the notes higher up is to use the left-hand octave shape.

Try putting finger 1 on any note on the third or fourth string – say A at fret two, string three – and at the same time place finger 4 two strings and three frets higher (at fret five on the first string). So now you're playing two A notes, an octave apart – in other words an octave interval. This shape can be moved up and down the fingerboard, so when you learn the lower note, you know the upper one too.

The pattern is the same when finger 1 is on strings three or four, but changes on strings five and six – here the upper octave note is only two strings and *two* frets away, and is played with finger 3. These patterns using notes G and A-sharp/B-flat are highlighted on the fingerboard (right).

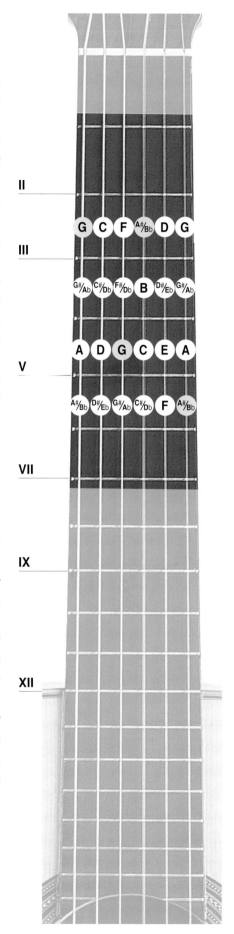

Fingerboard showing the notes at third position.

SECTION FOUR
PLAY CLASSICAL GUITAR

Tempo – part two

As well as the terms discussed earlier, you'll come across many others within the general repertoire. For example "lento e tranquillo", which means slow and tranquil; "con brio", meaning with vigour; or "acc", short for "accelerando", an indication to increase tempo. This last one is usually seen with a dotted line showing the section affected by the instruction.

EXERCISE 84 *This exercise makes use of the third position, both for normal playing and also for holding a half-barre at bar four in line two. The key is B-flat (two flats) though many accidentals are also used, especially towards the end of the piece.*

EXERCISE 85 *The exercise on the next page incorporates many of the techniques learnt so far, such as ligado, chords, intervals, position change and ties. The piece proceeds by developing different aspects of music used in the first line: for example, the theme in the first bar provides the rhythm of a quaver and two semiquavers (and the reverse) used throughout the first half of the piece. The quaver movement used in the first two notes and, more clearly, crossing bars three and four, also provides a steady pulse for the harmonic development in the last two lines of the piece. It's vital you are aware of the construction of any piece of music you are playing, and the musical material from which it's made – this makes interpreting a particular work much clearer. The chords in this*

*work are best played with **p** only, with the exception of the three-note chord at the end of line two which is to be arpeggiated with **p**, **i**, and **a**. "Dolce" at the start means "sweet", also implying "soft". "Rubato", in the last bar of line four, literally means "robbed" – in musical terms it lets you "steal" some extra time at this point to emphasise the phrase (in this case the third beat of the bar). When using rubato the sense of flow must not be stopped, just held up for a moment.*

SECTION FOUR
Full-barre

The full-barre is played the same way as the half-barre except the finger goes across all six strings. It's important to keep the "barring" finger completely straight and the left thumb well back behind the neck.

At first the full-barre feels quite tricky, but just remember it is usually combined with other fingers and is rarely needed to hold down all six strings by itself.

The symbol on the stave for a full-barre is a C followed by the Roman numeral indicating the position – just like the half-barre but without the ½ before it.

The chord in the left-hand diagram above (G) is a typical major chord shape using the full-barre (it's basically an E-chord shape moved up three frets with a barre across the third fret). In this case the sixth, second and first strings are the only ones fully held down by the barre.

The minor version of this chord (to its right) can be made by removing finger 2, leaving the finger 1 barre to hold down the B-flat instead of the B-natural held by finger 2.

EXERCISE 86 *(See top of next page.) The G minor chord above is used in bars one and six of Exercise 86. In bar two, the full-barre is reduced to covering only five strings. The chord making up the notes of the last beat of bar four is exactly the same shape as that at the beginning of the bar, but at a higher position: this should be used to your advantage – when playing beat three (with finger 4) the original chord played with 2, 1 and 3 is kept on, so when going to the higher position, finger 4 is simply removed and the whole shape is moved up. In the penultimate bar, **p** plays three consecutive bass strings: the easiest way to do this is to use apoyando on the first two so the thumb is already on the adjacent string ready to play. The instruction "a tempo", seen at the beginning of the third line, means "return to the original tempo" after the "rit" in the previous bar.*

Ligado – part two

Slurring down, as previously mentioned, is somewhat more difficult than slurring up – the left-hand finger is required to actually pluck the string slightly as it comes off the note. In Example 1, below, there is a slur from A to G: as with slurring up, the first note is played by the right hand, which, as well as sounding the A, provides enough energy in the string to help the left hand make it sound.

Example 2 is a slur from C to B using finger 1. This is slightly harder because it's nearer the nut, where the strings are less easy to move. When slurring down you must come off the string quite quickly otherwise the string will be damped. As with ligado going up, slurring down can be done with any fingers, even from 4 to 3, which is sometimes necessary if the other fingers are holding an interval or are part of a chord.

Slurs of three notes and more (see bottom diagram) can be made when a smooth passage between a number of notes is needed, or for a very high-speed sequence. Both types of ligado – up and down – are often combined, especially when playing "ornaments" (which we'll discuss later in this Section).

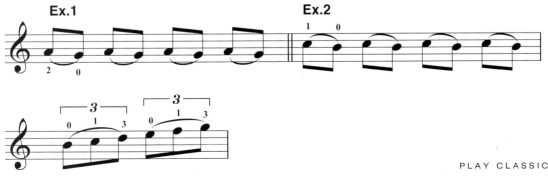

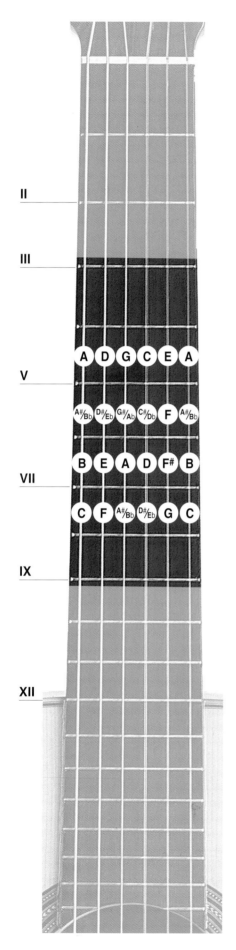

Fifth position (V)

The fifth position is particularly useful: first of all you can reach much higher notes on the first string – especially those a perfect 5th and minor 6th away from the open strings – which considerably expands melodic and harmonic possibilities. Also, finger 3 now covers the seventh fret, which is where the octave above the adjacent (lower) open string is found – for example the note at fret seven on the fifth string is E, an octave above the open sixth string. (Except on the second string, where the octave G is found at fret eight – played with finger 4 in fifth position – due to the major third between the G and B strings.)

The fifth position is a common place for the use of both the half and full-barre, especially in the keys of A and A minor.

At this position there is also a noticeable change in tone from the notes played lower down the fingerboard. For example, the D at fret seven on the third string has a far richer sound than the same D at fret III on string two, especially when played apoyando.

The distinct difference in tone colour found at the higher positions on the guitar is one the instrument's unique qualities – many pieces in the guitar repertoire use these positions for precisely this reason. One very famous example is the main theme in the slow movement of the *Concierto de Aranjuez* by Rodrigo, which would sound very cold and dry if played at the first position.

As with position III, learning each fret separately – and also making use of the left-hand octave shape – will help considerably in getting to know the notes in this position. The octave shape is especially useful, as it means the note played with finger 1, such as A at fret five on the sixth string, is the same as the next open string, which you're already familiar with – so once again one note helps you learn another.

Fingerboard showing the notes at fifth position.

'Cross String Jig' is played almost entirely in the fifth position. The right-hand fingering is of special importance in this piece as it facilitates the use of the open treble strings as an accompaniment. This happens from bar nine where **p** is used to play the top part and the fingers play the bass. The previously mentioned left-hand octave shape is used at the start of bar one.

EXERCISE 87

Ornaments

Ornaments (or "grace notes") are – as the name suggests – decorations added to the music by either composer or performer, depending on style, period of music and/or convention. Most ornaments originate in the Baroque period, and are also widely used in the music of the Classical and Romantic periods.

The ornaments most commonly used are: the acciaccatura, mordent (upper and lower), appoggiatura, turn, and trill.

Acciaccatura

The Acciaccatura (it literally means "crushed in") is a very fast note played just before the main one (and indicated by a tiny note with a line through its stem). Sometimes there are two or more notes, making a double or triple acciaccatura (see below, left). These are played as quickly as possible so the main note still arrives exactly at the place shown on the stave. If the grace note is on the same string, it should be slurred onto the main note (as below, right).

Mordent

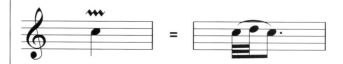

From the Italian word "mordere" (meaning "to bite"), this ornament is an extra note added in either above ("upper mordent") or below ("lower") the main note in order to reinforce it (adding extra *bite*, as it were). It's played with a three-note slur. Both types of mordent are indicated by a special jagged symbol (originally a stylised M) written above the note where it's to be played; the lower mordent symbol is differentiated by a small vertical line going through it (as seen below).

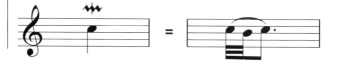

If the ornament note itself is to be a sharp or flat not already indicated by the key signature of the piece, then an accidental is written above or under the mordent symbol (depending on whether it's an upper or lower mordent).

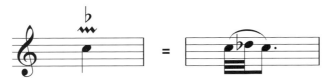

Appoggiatura

Another Italian term, this time referring to a "leaning" note, and shown by a miniature note symbol on the stave before the main note. In contrast to the more fleeting acciaccatura, the appoggiatura takes exactly half the rhythmic value of the main note (the one it "leans" into), or two thirds if the main note is dotted. As with all ornaments the appoggiatura is to be slurred, unless it involves crossing the strings.

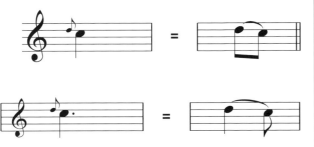

If attached to a tied note the appoggiatura takes the rhythmic value of the whole of the first of the tied notes.

When the appoggiatura comes before a chord, it affects only the top note of the chord, coming together with the chord itself then resolving onto the original top note by itself.

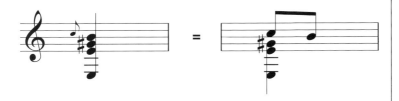

SECTION FOUR
PLAY CLASSICAL GUITAR

Turn

A turn is a short pattern of four notes used to make a small flourish from one note to the next. The order of notes to be played is: the note above the first main note, then the note itself, then the note below, and finally the note itself again.

The curly symbol indicating a turn can be in one of two places: if it's written above the first note, the turn occurs on that beat (as above); if it's written after the note, it's played between the two notes (as below).

The "inverted turn" (with a line through the symbol) is similar, except it begins on the note *below* the main one.

Trill

A trill is an extended alternation between the main (written) note and the note above it, and is denoted by the symbol "tr", often followed by a wavy line (usually indicating the length of trill). It is played as a long, seamless series of left-hand slurs.

In music up to and including the Classical period (for instance Haydn and Mozart), the trill starts on the upper note. In music since then the trill usually starts on the lower note. In much 20th century and later music the trill often has a small note attached (as with an acciaccatura) indicating which note to begin on.

As with the mordent, if a sharp or flat note is required as the upper note, this is indicated with an accidental above the symbol.

The trill is sometimes ended with a turn – if required, this is usually written in to avoid any ambiguity.

Another way to play a trill on the guitar is to have the two notes on adjacent strings. In this case it can be played with either **m** and **p** or with **a**, **m**, **i** and **p** – where **a** and **i** play the upper string and **m** and **p** play the lower.

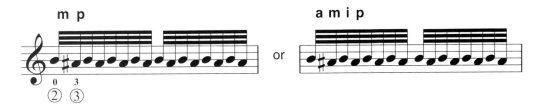

PLAY CLASSICAL GUITAR
SECTION FIVE

Scales

Time signatures – part 2

Seventh position (VII)

Nails

Vibrato

Harmonics

General musicianship

Sight-reading

Ninth position (IX)

Tremolo

Scales

Scales are practised on an instrument for two main reasons. The first and most obvious is for technical development, like refining the co-ordination between the hands, increasing playing speed, and to keep the volume and tone consistent.

The other purpose of scales is the practical application of theory within the tonal system of music. It's similar to the use of chords in understanding harmony.

The major and harmonic minor scales of each key contain all the notes used in the triads of that key.

These scales should be practised with both tirando and apoyando, initially with **m**, **i** as written, but also with **i**, **m**. The combinations of **a**, **i**, and **i**, **a** should be practised too.

C major scale - one octave.

The C minor harmonic scale below goes into sixth position (VI) on the fourth beat of bar one for ease of fingering. Although this position has not been covered, the given fingering and string numbering will make it clear enough. The only unusual note position is the A-flat at fret nine.

In bar two the B-flat is raised a semitone to B-natural to satisfy the harmonic requirement that the 7th note is a semitone below the Tonic. In minor keys this has to be done with an accidental, because they take their key signature from the major key that they're related to.

C minor harmonic scale – one octave.

SECTION FIVE
PLAY CLASSICAL GUITAR

The melodic minor scale is, as the name implies, used mainly for the melodic (or linear) aspect of music. This is mainly because its intervals are easier to sing than those of the harmonic minor scale.

In this scale there's a smooth transition up and down, with the major 2nd as the largest interval, whereas the harmonic minor has a minor 3rd leap between the 6th and 7th degrees of the scale.

To avoid the leap of a minor 3rd, the melodic minor scale uses different notes ascending than it does when descending.

C minor melodic scale – one octave.

Now we come to scales covering two octaves. Below are the scales of G, G minor harmonic and G minor melodic. These longer scales will take a bit more time to learn thoroughly but will prove to be very useful as these patterns can be moved up the fingerboard to make scales in different keys. For example moving the G major pattern up to position IV will give you A major.

G major scale – two octaves.

G minor harmonic scale – two octaves.

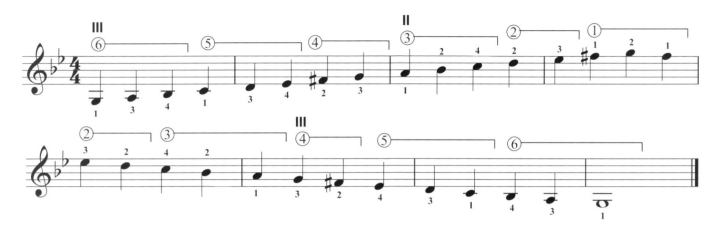

G minor melodic scale – two octaves.

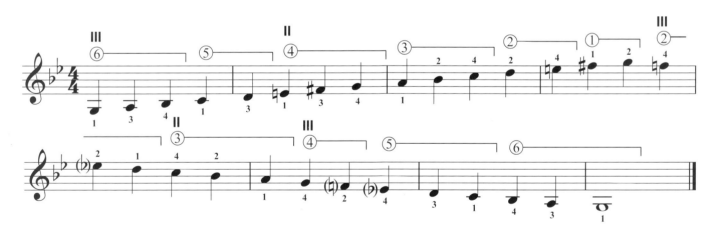

SECTION FIVE
PLAY CLASSICAL GUITAR

The chromatic scale uses every semitone in the octave and does not belong to any particular key. It takes its name from the Greek word chroma, meaning colour – with the implication that, because every note is used, it has a more "colourful" sound than the scales which are bound to one particular key.

The chromatic scale seen below goes up and down three octaves and a major 3rd from E to G-sharp and back – this means fingers 1 to 4 (and back) are used on every string.

Chromatic scale – starting on E.

Time signatures – part two

The time signature of $\frac{3}{8}$ is analogous to $\frac{3}{4}$, but the unit is a quaver instead of a crotchet. It's often used for brisk, dance-like music.

And $\frac{9}{8}$ is an interesting time signature, as it has three groups of three, in the same way that $\frac{6}{8}$ has two groups of three. In fact $\frac{9}{8}$ is similar to having a time signature of $\frac{3}{4}$ with a quaver triplet on every beat.

Note that $\frac{12}{8}$ works in the same way as $\frac{9}{8}$ but has four groups of three rather than three. Indeed $\frac{12}{8}$ is similar to $\frac{4}{4}$, but with a quaver triplet on every beat.

Seventh position (VII)

This position – like II, III and V – is of primary importance on the guitar. As mentioned in the section on the fifth position, fret VII is the octave point for the next lowest open string (and as such can also be used for tuning purposes). Also, a note at position VII is a perfect 5th higher than the open string – and, if you recall the discussion of chords in Section Four, this is both the third note of the triad and the dominant of the key. For example, on the third string the note at fret VII is D (the G triad is made up of G, B and D).

As with position III and V, both the half and full-barre are often used at position VII – for example the barre chord G at fret three, discussed in Section Four, can be moved up to position VII to make the chord of B.

At position VII finger 4 covers the tenth fret – so once you're fully familiarised with this position there's only the 11th fret left to learn (fret 12, where the neck meets the body, marks the octave point for each string, and the fingerboard begins again, with the 13th fret corresponding to fret one, the 14th to fret two, and so on to the end of the neck, the 19th fret).

When playing in the higher positions it's quite easy to accidentally make a note sound rather sharp by pushing the string out of its position. You can avoid this by ensuring that the left-hand fingers come as vertically as possible onto the string.

By practising high position passages very slowly to begin with, the accuracy of the finger angle is improved, especially when crossing from one string to another.

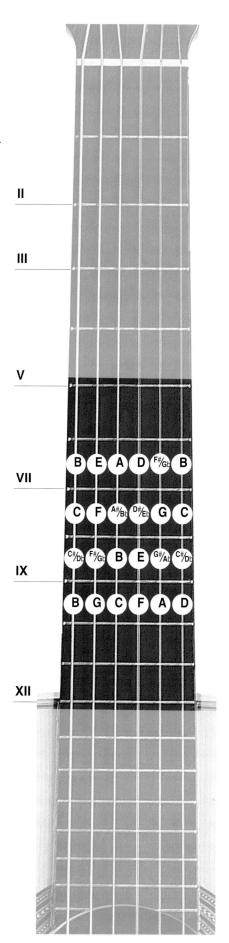

Fingerboard showing the notes at seventh position.

SECTION FIVE
PLAY CLASSICAL GUITAR

Glissando

A glissando is an audible slide from one note to another designed to give added expression to a melody or theme. Glissando is sometimes called "portamento", though strictly speaking portamento can only be done on those instruments without frets, such as the bowed string family or on some woodwind instruments. Glissando is usually indicated by the word "gliss" and a small line connecting the two notes. The finger stays on the string (still applying some pressure) and slides all the way from the first note to the second. This effect is well-suited to music from the Romantic period, or music in that style. Glissandi (plural) are also used in more recent styles of music, though in different ways – such as perhaps sliding entire chords up and down.

Usually the second note of a glissando is played but sometimes it is made to sound just by stopping at the required fret. This is most effective on the bass strings.

A small line connecting notes like this is usually used to mean a glissando, even if the word "gliss" or "port" does not appear. But when the line connects the *fingering* it means use a guide finger for changing position – although this stays on the string, it must not apply pressure or an unwanted slide may be audible.

EXERCISE 88

There is a glisssando in bar two of line three in this work. Most of this exercise is in seventh position. This piece is also suited to the use of vibrato, especially on held notes like the first melody note C. In the first bar of the last line there's a double slur – both notes are played simultaneously with the left hand only: this is not too difficult, but it's vital the two notes sound exactly together. It's also important in this piece that the bass notes are damped when not being used (as explained in Section Three), so the harmony is clear. The short line above the F-sharp at bar two of line three is called a "tenuto" mark (sometimes accompanied by the abbreviation "ten"), which means you should hold this note for a fraction longer than its value, though not as long as a fermata.

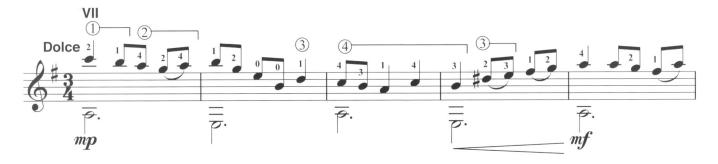

Nails

By this stage in the book your playing will have reached a level where we can start to think about developing projection and tone. A lot can be done to add clarity and shape to your sound by the correct use of the right-hand fingernails.

Your right-hand nails should be grown so they are just visible over the fingertips, when looking at the palm of the hand (see photo on the right).

The string isn't played with the nails as such, but rather with the fingertip and nail together. To do this properly, the shape of the nail is very important: to some extent it follows the contour of the fingertip, but it should be slightly flatter across the top so the nail isn't too long, which could make for a rather thin, weak sound.

The angle at which the fingertip and nail play the string can be clearly seen in the "finger-stroke" photographs in Section One.

Since everybody has different hands and finger lengths, there's no perfect nail shape to suit all players. Experiment to find your best, projecting tone, with minimum resistance when the fingernail meets the string, and then keep the nail shaped accordingly.

The underside of the nail, which is where the contact with the string is made, must be kept very smooth and evenly polished so there's no friction to either slow you down or distort your tone.

The best way of shaping the nails is to use a set of fine sandpapers or emery boards, getting progressively finer until finally polishing with a buffer. It helps if you file or sand the nail in the same direction as the movement of the string (diagonally across the nail – see photographs in Section One).

This photograph demonstrates the amount of nail that shows over the fingertip when it's the ideal length to produce a good tone. Note the shape too: the contour follows the fingertip with a slight flattening out across the top.

SECTION FIVE
PLAY CLASSICAL GUITAR

Vibrato

Vibrato is used to add some life and expression to your guitar-playing (in fact it's used on all stringed, and many other, instruments – including of course the original instrument, the human voice).

It involves subtly varying the pitch, up and down, either side of a note. This actually has the effect of focusing the listener's attention on the note in the middle, and generally increasing its emotional impact.

Vibrato is created by a controlled side-to-side motion of the left forearm and wrist, moving parallel to the guitar neck. This movement is then transmitted to the string through the focal point of the finger, "vibrating" behind the fret, effectively stretching and loosening the string by tiny amounts and producing the desired pitch variation (see the photograph on the opposite page).

Again it's vital the thumb is anchored solidly in position on the back of the neck, so the movement of the hand does not throw the finger out of position.

Although vibrato is often used on the first string, it works best on strings two to six, and in the higher positions. When attempting vibrato for the first time it's advisable to use a note on the second or third string at around fret seven.

Finger 2 is the easiest to use effectively, as it's directly opposite the thumb – but it's essential that each finger is able to produce a good vibrato.

In general vibrato is used when playing lines or notes that are either isolated or quite distinct from the bass or other parts – such as the theme in the piece 'Adelita' found in Section Six. When used together with apoyando, vibrato produces a very effective and characteristic guitar tone.

Vibrato can also be used in intervals, in other words on more than one string at a time. It generally works best in pieces where a note is held long enough for the effect to be heard. Vibrato is difficult to produce in chords (this technique is more suited to some forms of jazz), although it may be specifically called for as an extended technique in a contemporary piece.

Each player's vibrato speed is a personal part of his/her playing, though in practice the speed is strongly linked to the musical style and tempo of the piece being played – so be careful to judge it wisely. As a general guideline, the speed should be moderate: high-speed vibrato produces a rather frantic-sounding effect, and should be used only when specifically called for in a particular passage.

SECTION FIVE
PLAY CLASSICAL GUITAR

This picture indicates the movement of the fingertip, and hence the string, when producing a vibrato.

SECTION FIVE
PLAY CLASSICAL GUITAR

Harmonics

Harmonics on the guitar are special bell-like tones produced by touching a string at particular points along the fretboard, which effectively divides the length of the string into smaller sections.

There are two types of harmonic available on the guitar: the natural and the artificial. Natural harmonics are the easier of the two, so it's best to begin with these.

The most common harmonic is the octave, which is produced when the string is divided in half – the two halves of the string are ringing as two separate units, with the harmonic point (called a node) acting as a bridge or point of non-movement.

To produce the octave harmonic, place any left-hand finger lightly on the sixth string, exactly above the 12th fret (the nodal point for this harmonic), but don't press the string onto the fingerboard. Next, pluck the string while the left-hand finger is still in place, then remove it to allow the note to ring.

The resulting note in this case is an E one octave above the open string. (Note that harmonics ring most clearly if the right hand plays closer to the bridge than usual.)

Harmonics produced at other frets – where the string is divided into parts of differing lengths, and therefore pitches – are less predictable to the uninitiated. For example, on the fifth string, where playing "standard" notes at frets five, seven, nine and 12 would usually result in the sequence D, E, F-sharp, A, the harmonics struck at the same frets produce A, E, C-sharp, A.

Harmonics are usually notated by diamond-shaped note-heads on the stave, and in guitar notation accompanied by Roman numerals indicating fret. Notation methods vary, though: sometimes you are given the open-string note with the position where you'd find the required harmonic on that string; sometimes you're told the harmonic note to be played (which is not necessarily the note that sounds, as we've seen); and sometimes you are given the resulting note itself. This last one is the most rational – you're told the note which actually sounds, together with the position and string number, so there is no ambiguity. It also means you don't lose the visual contour of the music on the page.

You will often see an abbreviation of the word harmonic (armonico in Italian), such as "harm" or "arm", written above the harmonic note in the score. This is also sometimes accompanied by "nat" or "art" indicating whether it's a natural or artificial harmonic.

The diagram on the next page shows the natural harmonics found on the sixth string using the notation discussed above. You can see that the order of the intervals above the open string is: octave, octave + perfect 5th (12th), two octaves (15th), two octaves + major 3rd (17th), two octaves + perfect 5th.

In this photograph, finger 4 on the left hand is touching the node above fret XII on the top string, producing the harmonic E an octave above the open string. Note that the right hand is playing closer to the bridge than usual: this is very effective when playing harmonics, greatly enhancing their volume and clarity.

This set of intervals (plus higher inaudible ones) is known as the harmonic series and is a phenomenon of nature present in all sound, musical and non-musical.

This pattern of intervals is the same on all strings in relation to the particular note of the open string (which is known as the fundamental or first harmonic).

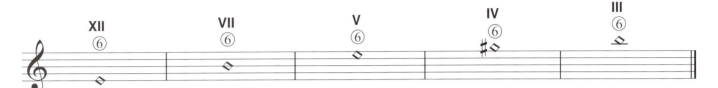

Artificial harmonics

These are called "artificial" because the fundamental note of the string is changed (by holding it at a fret with the left hand), so any harmonics produced are not the naturally occurring harmonics of that string.

The essential idea of the division of the string remains, it's just that the overall length of the string is shortened. This allows harmonics to be produced that are otherwise unavailable using only the open strings.

There is one complication, of course: the fact that the left-hand is being used to fret a note means the right hand has to do the two jobs of holding the harmonic node and then plucking the string (as in the photographs below).

Photograph 1 shows the **i** finger touching the nodal point over the high B on string one (fret 19). In photograph 2 the **a** finger is seen preparing to pluck the first string. In photograph 3 the **a** finger has played the first string and the **i** finger is just leaving the note, allowing the harmonic to sound.

In the Example below, the **i** finger is on the fourth string exactly above the 15th fret, with the left-hand finger 3 holding the note F. After plucking this note (with **a**) the left hand then holds an E and the right-hand **i** finger follows it down to the 14th fret. Finally there's an open D (natural harmonic) which, to avoid making a huge jump with the left hand, can also be played as an artificial harmonic, using **i** to hold the nodal point on the string.

General musicianship

Although learning the guitar is your principle aim, to be a good guitarist you also need to be a good musician. Instrumental technique must be reinforced by the physical and mental skills known as musicianship.

This rather wide-sounding term encompasses only a few essentials:

▍ Physical awareness of rhythm and tempo and the ability to hear these in your mind.
▍ The ability to reproduce heard music on your instrument without the aid of a score.
▍ Sight-reading of a score at a tempo close to that of actual performance. This allows you to get to know a great deal of music without having to refer to recordings.
▍ Ensemble playing – this includes skills like keeping in time with other musicians, blending/contrasting tone colour, following a conductor, and accompaniment technique (the ability to follow rapid movement and change in a soloist's part).

If you plan to make guitar-playing a career, you also need a professional attitude, and some social skills – basically a flexibility in approach that allows you to work with all kinds of people and still get the best musical results.

There isn't one definitive way to improve musicianship: there are courses and books (such as Paul Hindemith's *Training for Musicians*, Schott & Co, 1946), or you can just learn by experience.

The ideal is a combination of all of these, but there is a lot you can do to help yourself.

Physical awareness of rhythm can be enhanced by a disciplined approach to beat-counting and hearing a pulse in the mind, especially when you're first learning the instrument.

Playing with other musicians is also a major factor in good rhythm sense, as players must keep a steady rhythm to stay in time with each other.

(The style of music played in an ensemble can affect the development of an acute rhythmic sense. Those with some experience of playing jazz and some forms of popular music will find this a great advantage when coming to play classical guitar duets/trios, or accompanying singers).

Learning music without a score, or "by ear", is an essential skill for a performer, as it gives you a more direct and natural connection with the instrument. Although classical players have had a somewhat bad reputation for only being able to play from a score, this began to change in the last decades of the 20th century, due to a widening range of styles of music played by trained musicians. This trend is reflected by the fact that most major music colleges now have compulsory courses in reproducing heard music and improvisation.

From the 16th century up to the mid 19th century the majority of performers were all-round musicians, who were also composers. This meant improvisation was an essential skill, as they were often called upon to provide unwritten accompaniment (such as the continuo parts played by lutenists and harpsichordists), or to make up their own cadenzas in concertos.

When you are attempting to learn a piece or theme from a recording, try to work out one phrase and then make a mental note of what the relationship is between the notes. This will highlight any recurrent or dominating pitch, which will indicate a key signature.

The primary chords of the two keys (E and C) shown at the start of Section Four provide a basic framework of the tonal system. But since the early 20th century other musical systems have appeared, as all the combinations within the existing tonal system began to be overused. These include serialism, bi-tonality, modality and aleatorism – all of which have their own rules of progression and growth based on parameters other than the key system of tonality. (Music written with these systems is generally Art music, and is still only beginning to form a background language that can be picked up by ear.)

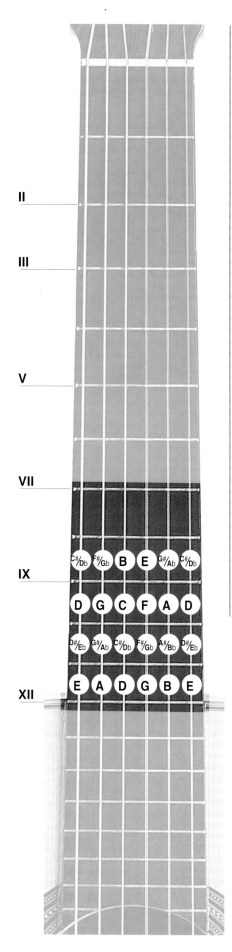

Sight-reading

Good sight-reading can be achieved gradually by daily practice. Choose pieces well within your playing ability, so the only variable is the reading itself. Short works are the best; music colleges often publish sight-reading exercises graded according to ability.

The main points to remember about sight-reading are:
- Look over the piece for a minute before playing and try to spot any places where difficulties may occur, such as position changes or accidentals.
- Keep going, even if you make a mistake.
- Maintain a steady tempo (choose a tempo suitable for your ability and err on the side of caution). Sight-reading *must* be done in "real time", as if it is a performance, and not "step time" as when you're learning a piece.

If you're strict with your sight-reading practice, eventually you'll be able to read from a score at close to performance tempo.

Ninth position (IX)

Position IX is important not only because it completes the fingerboard, but it's also another very commonly used position – finger 4 plays the 12th fret here (the octave point).

(Other positions such as IV, VI, VIII and X have not been covered in specific lessons because they are covered by the combination of the main positions, and their use will be self-evident in pieces where they appear.)

The picture on the left shows the notes at ninth position.

The piece on the next page, Exercise 89, makes use not only of position IX, but positions II, VII and others. The notes played in the ninth position should present no problem, as all the necessary fingering is given. The harmonics in this piece are designed to help you move from one position to another as, like open strings, they will continue to ring when the left hand is moved away. The sudden dynamic changes at bar two of line three and the start of line four are especially effective if the shifts in volume are done promptly. The trill at the end starts on the lower note, in keeping with the Classical style of the piece. The instruction "piú mosso" in line five means literally "more movement" (increase the tempo), while "meno mosso" ("less movement") in line six means the reverse – slow down.

EXERCISE 89

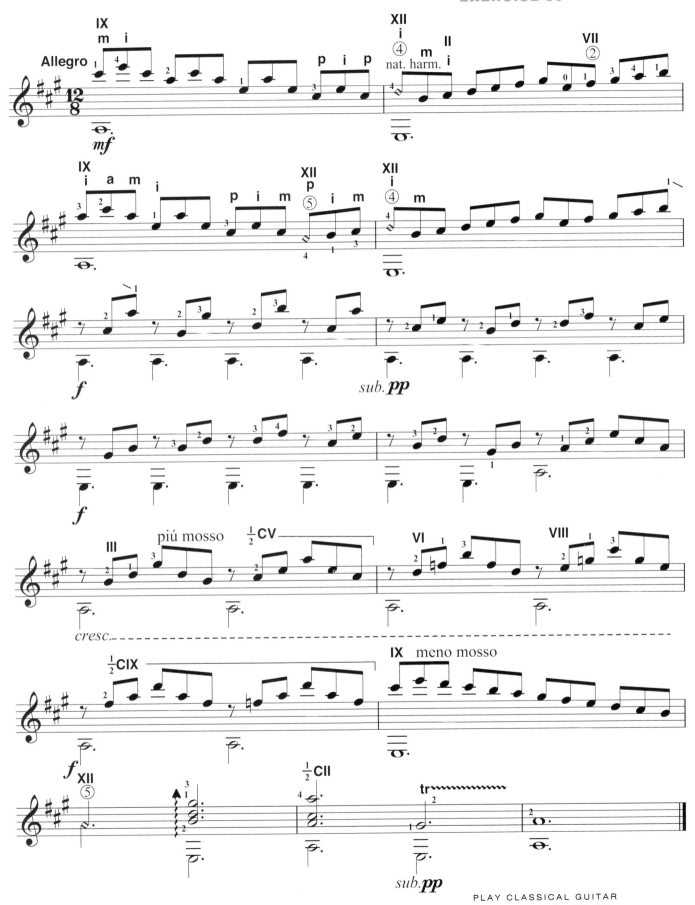

SECTION FIVE
PLAY CLASSICAL GUITAR

Tremolo

The classical guitar is not capable of producing long, sustained notes in the way that, say, a violin or oboe can. Even the open bass strings, which inevitably produce the longest notes, have a rather short delay time.

This characteristic of the instrument is not a disadvantage – if it wasn't the case, complex music would not be possible, as you'd waste a great deal of concentration and energy on damping unwanted sustaining strings. (Indeed if you've ever tried to play classical guitar repertoire on an electric guitar, which has a much longer sustain, this problem becomes immediately evident.)

An impression of a held line can be produced by the use of tremolo. Tremolo is basically a single note repeated several times at high speed – a technique that may be familiar from its use on the mandolin, for example. (Guitarists moving across from the rock genre should be careful not to confuse tremolo with vibrato – which, as we discussed earlier, describes a fluctuation of pitch.)

Tremolo is played using the right-hand **a**, **m**, and **i** fingers on the relevant string, with the thumb, **p**, playing the bass after every stroke of the **i** finger, so there's a continuous cycle of **p**, **a**, **m**, and **i**. This can be seen in the example below:

The difficulty with tremolo is achieving a high speed without sacrificing good tone or volume in the upper part – and perhaps most importantly keeping a smooth continuous movement.

Tremolo is made up of two things: four separate finger movements and an overall continuous cycle – which at high speed are perceived as one movement. The four finger movements must each have a full sound and must not be cut short by the subsequent note.

It should be pointed out that the tremolo is one of the most difficult guitar techniques, and will take a long time to perfect. As with all technical aspects of guitar, slow practice is essential at the beginning so you can pay attention to legato movement and consistency of tone and volume.

Repetitive techniques such as tremolo are often required to run continuously for a number of minutes – as in repertoire pieces like 'Recuerdos de la Alhambra' by Francisco Tárrega (1852-1909).

It's important the right arm stays relaxed while developing this technique, especially when beginning to increase the tempo. When things are played fast before you're comfortably ready, tension can easily creep in to the proceedings and gradually seize up the movement, making you grind to a halt.

Practise the four finger movements fairly slowly, and try to keep going for as long as is constructive without increasing the tempo. By speeding up too early you can actually undo the work already done. After a period of regular practice (ideally every day), the movement will begin to feel more comfortable. At this point it can be nudged to a slightly higher tempo, though not at the expense of regular and smooth movement. If the technique is gradually developed this way, a relatively fast tempo can be reached while the pattern is still perceived as four separate movements. At this stage you can try the next step to a smooth tremolo.

In a good tremolo it will seem as if the consecutive movements are triggered from the hand in one go, rather than from the brain as four separate instructions. At this point your mind is working at a higher level of control, with the attention focused on overseeing the whole movement rather than the local mechanics, which will have already been "programmed" during the slow practice. The speed of a true tremolo is quick enough so the four-note element of the cycle becomes inaudible to the listener – the brain is tricked into perceiving a sustained line.

SECTION FIVE
PLAY CLASSICAL GUITAR

EXERCISE 90

This exercise on the following two pages is designed to develop the tremolo alongside the use of the left hand. At bar seven and eight the tremolo is played on the inner strings, which can be tricky at first as there's less room to move. At the fourth beat of bar three, the top of the barre (the tip of the left-hand finger) must be lifted so the open A can be played on the next beat. At the end of bar nine finger 4 is used as a guide to slide up to the high C-sharp in bar ten. All the half-barres used in the last three lines must reach up to the fourth string to hold down the notes on that string.

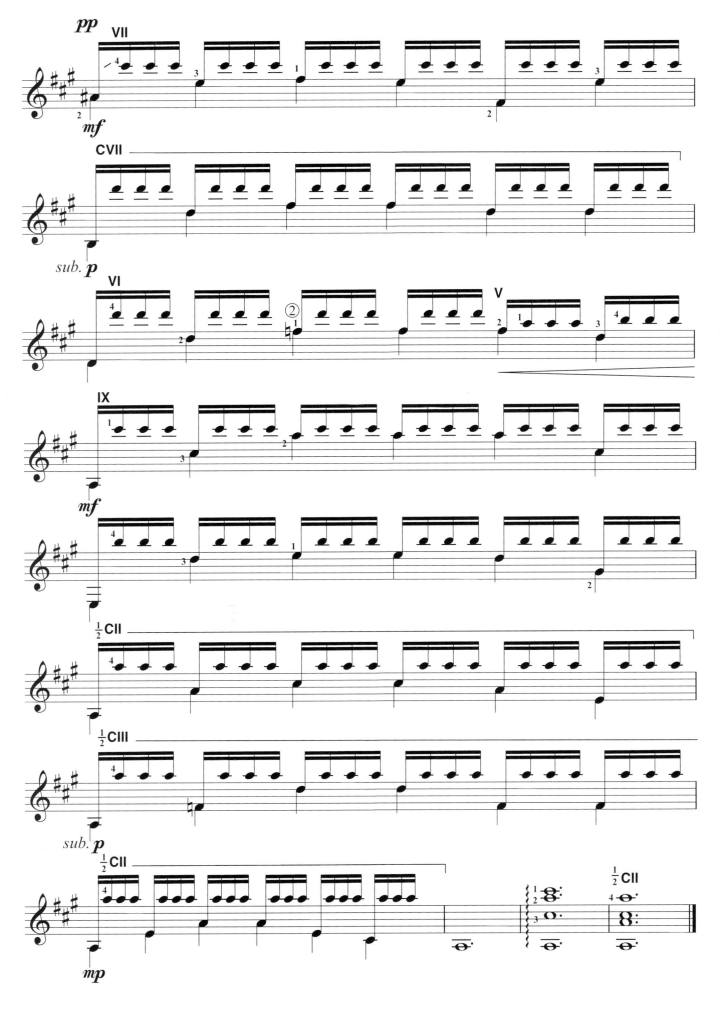

EXERCISE 91 — *Study No9 from 'Melodic & Progressive Studies Opus 60' by Matteo Carcassi (1792–1853). Although this piece is not a tremolo work, the main right-hand pattern is the same as that used for tremolo and will help to develop its use in a musical context containing other patterns. In this piece it is essential that the two lines made by the bass and top notes of the arpeggio are distinct. First of all make sure the bass notes are always held for their written length, so they connect together to make a continuous line. Do the same with the top part. For example, in bar two the F at the top of the first chord must be held right up to the E (the third semiquaver of beat two). This effect can also be clearly heard in bar one of line six as the top G moves to the F-sharp, the F and finally to the open E in bar two. The word "poco" in bar two of line four means "a little" – in this case a little "rit".*

SECTION FIVE
PLAY CLASSICAL GUITAR

PLAY CLASSICAL GUITAR
SECTION SIX

Tone colour

Scales (part 2)

Hemi & demisemiquavers

Extended techniques

Four study pieces

Examples of guitar repertoire

Historical overview of repertoire

Guide to buying a classical guitar

Tone colour

Tone colour, or timbre, is a way of explaining the type of sound produced by a musical instrument. Adjectives such as bright, warm, dark, thin and so on are often used to describe a particular tone or "colour" of sound.

The timbre of any sound depends on several factors: the way it's produced; how many parts or notes are involved; the attack at the beginning of the sound; and also, to an extent, even its volume and pitch.

The guitar is capable of a wide range of tone colour, depending on where the string is played by the right hand and the position of the note held by the left hand. As mentioned already, the use of the higher left-hand positions give a warmer sound than the lower ones, as well as a much better response to vibrato.

With the right hand, the basic tone depends largely on the nail shape, the way the finger follows through after playing the string, and whether you are playing tirando or apoyando.

More unusual colours can be produced by moving the playing position of the right hand. If the string is played quite close to the bridge, a hard, bright sound is produced – this is called "ponticello" or "sul pont" ("on the bridge" in Italian). Various degrees of brightness can be obtained, depending on how close to the bridge you go. Even a slight movement in this direction from the usual playing position (which is over the soundhole) will change the tone to an extent.

Conversely, moving in the other direction, so your right hand is playing near or over the end of the fretboard, will produce a softer, warmer sound, and is written as "sul tasto" ("on the fingerboard").

You can achieve an interesting sound on the bass strings – not unrelated to sul tasto – when the right hand is exactly 12 frets (one octave) away from the left hand. The fact that the harmonic node is at this point results in a rather hollow sound being produced.

As with all variables – such as dynamics and tempo fluctuations – tone colour should be modified sparingly, and is best used to underline structural points in the music. A good example is when a phrase is immediately repeated – the second time could be played "sul pont", at a *pp* dynamic to highlight the repeat.

Section Six: Scales – part two

As with those in Section Five, the following scales should be practised using both tirando and apoyando, first with **m**, **i** as written, but also with **i**, **m**, plus the combinations of **a**, **i**, and **i**, **a**.

Another right-hand fingering that should be learned is **a**, **m**, **i**. This can feel a little strange at first, but because the work is shared between three fingers it can be used to achieve very high speed.

Below are the two-octave scales of C and C minor beginning on the fifth string. The fingering pattern for these scales is especially worth learning, as it can be used in different positions to play other scales: for example, E major is found at the seventh fret (played at position VI because it starts with finger 2).

C major scale – two octaves.

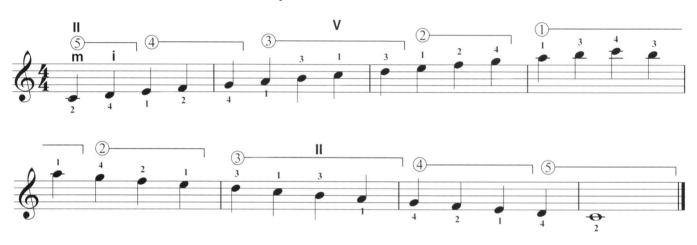

C minor harmonic scale – two octaves.

C minor melodic scale – two octaves.

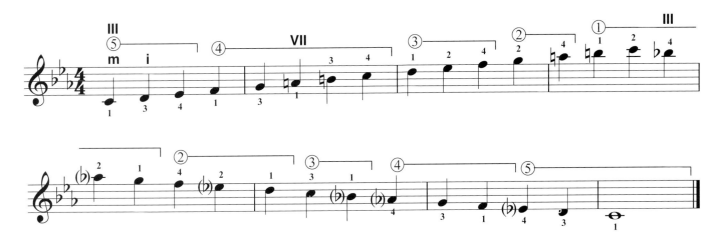

Three-octave scales begin on the sixth string and involve three different positions. The G major and two G minor scales shown on the next couple of pages make use of the 12th and 13th positions. These positions have not been covered specifically, but as previously mentioned the 12th position is the same as the first position, except an octave higher. So on the first string, F is at the 13th fret, G is at the 15th, and so on.

G major scale – three octaves.

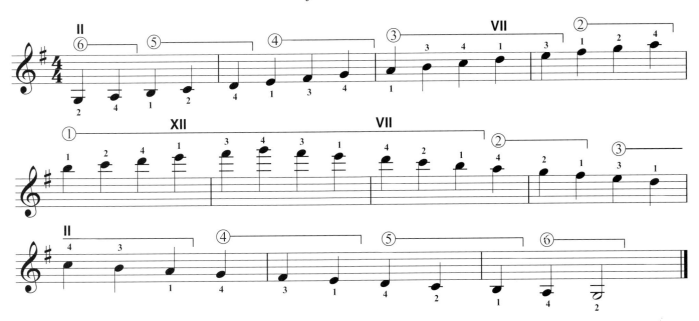

G minor harmonic scale – three octaves.

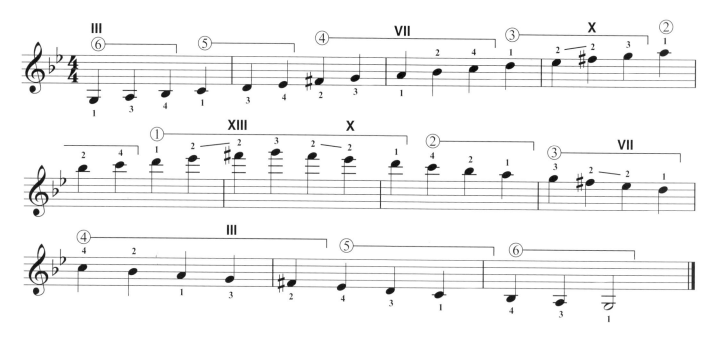

G minor melodic scale – three octaves.

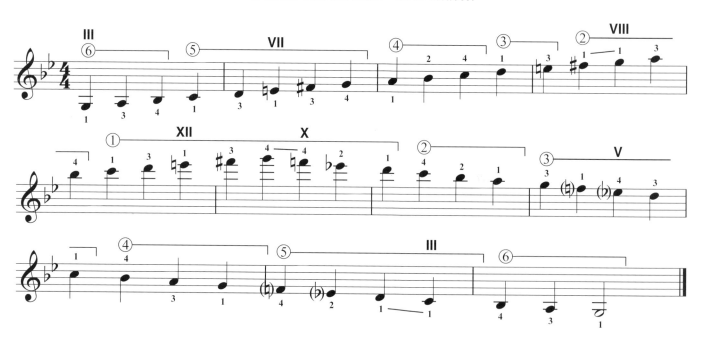

As well as the single-line scales dealt with already, scales can be in 3rds, 6ths, octaves and more unusual intervals. These types of scale are outside the scope of this book – you'd be advised to get one of the official scale books used for grade exams to widen this area of study. But on the next page you'll find one scale in octaves for reference, and also for its value as a left-hand exercise. The scale is E major, and is best approched by playing the octave notes separately at first. When the scale has been memorised you can progress to playing the octaves simultaneously.

It may look like there's a lot of position changes, but they are not large leaps. Together with the comfortable fingering, they allow for more ease of movement than if the position were more fixed – which would cause awkward and impractical fingering.

SECTION SIX
PLAY CLASSICAL GUITAR

E major scale in octaves.

Demi & hemidemisemiquavers

These are also known as 32nd and 64th notes respectively, and are usually only in pieces with a slow tempo (as in Exercise 92 below). The demisemiquaver (notated like a quaver, but with three tails) has half the value (ie is twice as quick) as a semiquaver. The hemidemisemiquaver (like a quaver with four tails) has only half of that value, which means there are 16 in a crochet.

There are four hemidemisemiquavers at the end of bar one, to be slurred together. Even though the A lands on a string which has not been played (the third) and so has no energy, the note can be made to sound quite easily by bringing the finger down quickly so the force on the string produces enough volume. The ornament on the last note is an appoggiatura G-sharp – it has the value of a semiquaver.

EXERCISE 92

PLAY CLASSICAL GUITAR
121

SECTION SIX
PLAY CLASSICAL GUITAR

Extended techniques

Extended techniques are unusual playing styles that are outside the "normal" use of the instrument, and have for the most part been developed in the last 100 years or so. Here is a selection of the most commonly used extended techniques.

Pizzicato

This is normally used as a direction to string players to pluck the string instead of using the bow. Although it may seem odd to apply this term to the guitar, which is usually plucked anyway, it's used to describe a special technique producing a sound similar to the plucked string on bowed instruments.

The result required in a good pizzicato is a short, damped note which still has a clear pitch. It's done by resting the heel of the right hand on the strings just in front of the bridge (see photographs below), which stops them ringing fully, and then plucking with the thumb (**p**) only, even on the treble strings.

Experiment to find the best hand position: if the note sounds too much like a dull thud with little pitch, the hand is too far to the left. Alternatively if the string is still ringing for a length of time, and the sound is similar to the usual tone, the hand is too far to the right, on the bridge, and is not damping the strings enough.

It's not possible to damp all the strings together: you have to get the hand in the best position to damp the string being played.

The photograph on the right shows a pizzicato being played on the A-string: the string is usually plucked by the bone on the left of the first thumb joint, though the flesh on the side of the thumb can also be used. The photograph below shows the angle of the hand from the front. Note that the thumb is parallel to the strings, with the fingers well out of the way.

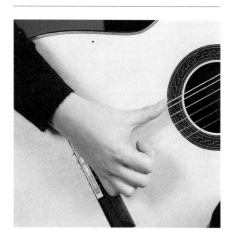

Tambor

The word tambor means "drum" in Spanish, and is a guitar technique used to give a different attack to the sound. It's done by using the left-hand side of **p** to hit against the strings – most effectively done about an inch from the bridge. Its effect is, as you'd expect, rather drum-like, and often used rhythmically.

Due to the interest in tone colour in much post-19th century music, effects like this have found their way into many works of the period: a good example is the *Sequenza XI for Guitar* by Luciano Berio (b1925), written for the guitarist Eliot Fisk in 1988.

Bartók or snap pizz

This is named after Hungarian composer Béla Bartók (1881-1945), who is sometimes credited with inventing this technique for string instruments. It's done by pulling the string between **p** and **i** away from the guitar and then quickly releasing it back on to the fretboard to make a loud snap. One very useful thing about this technique is that the pitch of the note can still be heard, which means entire phrases of music can be played using it. "Snap pizz" is especially effective on the guitar because of the metal frets, which add a powerful edge to the sound.

As this technique sounds very extreme, it is only to be used when actually indicated in the music.

The symbols are

Scordatura

Scordatura is when one or more strings are tuned to a different pitch than usual. The most common use is when the sixth string is taken down a tone to the note D. Another scordatura often used involves dropping the third string a semitone to F-sharp, which moves the major third from between strings three and two to strings four and three. This imitates the tuning pattern of a Renaissance lute, and is used for playing lute music on the guitar – such as the works of British composer John Dowland (1562–1626). Another tuning variation is when the fifth string is dropped a tone to G, along with the sixth string down to D, which changes the tonality of the open strings from the usual E minor to G. Instructions for scordatura are written at the beginning of a piece or movement in the manner of "6th to D".

SECTION SIX
PLAY CLASSICAL GUITAR

Campanella

Campanella means "little bell" in Italian, and is a technique which increases the resonance of the instrument by making use of the open strings to keep notes ringing as long as possible, and by playing each subsequent note on a different string. Not all sequences of notes can be played this way, but just doing part of a line will usually be enough to produce the desired effect.

The example below is a descending scale from the open E, and makes use of the harmonic A to increase the resonance further. By following the fingering and string numbers precisely the campanella sound will be achieved. The left-hand fingers must be held on as long as possible so the notes they are holding continue to sound when playing the subsequent note. This results in two or three notes sounding together which is what produces the campenella sound.

Four study pieces

Here are four final works for you to try out the various techniques and musical theory you've learned throughout the book.

The first piece is a study in thirds. The two notes of each interval (when they are both fretted notes) should be placed on the fingerboard together. The repeated right-hand pattern of **p, m, i** allows for a continuous smooth motion so you can concentrate on the left-hand position changes. Where there are chords, care must be taken to ensure all the notes in the chord are played exactly together and sound strong – this can be difficult at first because of the sudden change of right-hand function from arpeggio to chord, but it can be achieved by preparing the fingers on the strings for a moment, during slow practice, before playing the chord. In line four there's an almost constant change of position between each third, but if you notice that the left hand always plays either 3 and 2 or 3 and 1 (depending on whether the 3rd is minor or major), and the lower note stays on the second string until the beginning of line five, this should make finding the notes quite simple.

'Etude No 3, Opus 48' by Mauro Giuliani (1781–1828). STUDY PIECE 1

In the second piece, over the page, the notes with the stems up in the first line are the melody notes and must be brought out louder than the accompanying lower part. In lines three and four there is an extensive use of guide fingers between the position changes. These position changes are not marked because the bass notes and fingering do provide sufficient information about which positions are needed.

STUDY PIECE 2   *'Etude No 1, Opus 48' by Giuliani.*

The study on the next page, 'Adelita', is a very popular piece in the guitar repertoire, and is based on a Polish dance known as a mazurka. A work of this type relies largely on the clarity of the melody and the rhythmic flow.

This piece incorporates many of the techniques taught so far, such as ornaments (which are fully written out by the composer), ligado, and playing in various high positions. Apoyando should be used on the first and third notes of bars one, two and three to produce a strong, sweet sound.

In bar three the chord on the last beat, which in previous bars was an accompanying harmony, now has the melody note G as its top note. This note must be brought out louder than the rest of the chord by pushing the **m** finger further into the string then the **i**, and it should flow directly into the next bar. Such crossover between melody and accompaniment also occurs later in the piece

– for instance on the final beat of all the bars in line three. In the first bar of line four there is quite a stretch between fingers 3 and 4 (the ornament), which will need to be practised very slowly at first.

In the second bar of line four the melody is now in the tenor voice and must be brought into relief by emphasis of the right-hand finger stroke. A short glissando in the next bar from the high G to the D will heighten the cantabile, or singing, quality of the piece. The first note of all the ornaments must be played simultaneously with the chord. The use of vibrato in this piece is very characteristic and will bring the work to life – it is especially effective when used in the top line of the first half of the piece, and also later when the theme is on the bass strings in the second bar of line four.

SECTION SIX
PLAY CLASSICAL GUITAR

'Adelita' by Francisco Tárrega (1852–1909). **STUDY PIECE 3**

SECTION SIX
PLAY CLASSICAL GUITAR

Study piece four, opposite, while not technically very difficult to play, relies on interpretation and understanding of the style for a successful performance.

Accents on the beat are to be avoided, to emphasise the linear movement, and the pulse should always be pushed onwards to produce a lyrical and rather floating quality.

This piece was written for the vihuela, a Spanish Renaissance instrument. It has a similar tuning to the guitar, except that, like the Renaissance lute, the major 3rd falls between strings three and four rather than two and three as on the guitar. In order to play this music with a suitable fingering a scordatura is used, dropping the third string to F-sharp.

A capo (a small, clamp-like device fixed on the neck which stops all the strings at a certain fret), can be used here at the third fret to bring the pitch of the guitar to G, the same as the viheula. (Having said this, accepted concert pitch has risen considerably since the 16th century, so it may be that our modern F is closer to the G used at that time, rendering the use of a capo unnecessary.)

The instrumental music of this period imitates the vocal style closely, with the linear aspect of the music dominating. As a result great care must be taken to emphasise the melodic movement.

For example: in bar two, line two, the bass E must be damped when going to the A so the interval is heard melodically and so that the two notes do not ring together, which would cause harmonic ambiguity.

The linear aspect is obvious again in the "imitation" in line two, between bars one and three, where the bass motif is repeated a 4th higher. This also happens in the subsequent bar another 4th higher, but with the first note missing for variation. Also, the contour of the top part of bar one, line two, is repeated on the bass in the next bar, but with different intervals because of the new harmonic function required at this point.

There's a lot of fingering given on the stave, due to the unfamiliarity caused by the scordatura. How a player fingers a piece is based largely on experience, as it depends so much on context, but a good guide is to remember that it should always be comfortable. Other parameters, such as position change and where the left-hand thumb is placed, can have enormous consequences.

The dynamics on this piece are editorial only, and are simply a suggestion for the type of gradual change suited to this style.

The indication "despacio" at the beginning means "slowly" in Spanish, but a certain amount of movement is needed to keep the piece flowing along. The tempo given is an approximation, and should help give the piece a sense of flow.

'Soneto II' by Enriquez de Valderrábano (1500–1557) **STUDY PIECE 4**

SECTION SIX
PLAY CLASSICAL GUITAR

Historical overview of repertoire

The repertoire for guitar goes back to the late 15th century in Spain when the instrument was developed for court use in favour of the lute, which had strong connotations with the recently banished Moors. The guitar at the time had four courses. Courses are sets of two identically tuned strings played together. Two more courses were added to make a new instrument, the "vihuela de mano" ("de mano", meaning "of the hand", signified that it was played with the fingers rather than a pick or quill, as were other vihuelas). By using the right-hand fingers independently, a much more sophisticated music was now playable than was possible with a plectrum, and the general growth of contrapuntal music at the time (largely sacred composition) meant that works for the new instrument flourished.

Composers such as Luis Milán (1500–1561) and Alonso Mudarra (c1510–1580) wrote very high quality pieces, still performed today, for both the vihuela de mano and four-course guitar – though the latter instrument found greater favour in France and Italy than it

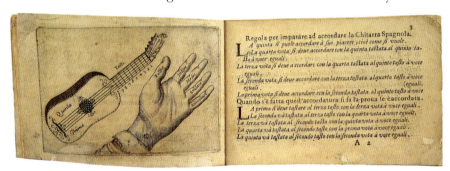

A two-page spread from the 16th century book El Maestro by Luisve Milan, showing the fret numbers on the instrument and the names of the fingers.

did in Spain, because of the absence of the competing vihuela. These works were generally published in collections, such as Milán's *El Maestro* (1535) which is a book of fantasias (free contrapuntal works). Another composer of the period, Luys de Narváez (c1490–c1560), arranged a number of vocal pieces by the celebrated French composer Josquin Desprez (c1440–1521), adding inventive variations which took the instrument's technique to new levels.

By the end of the 16th century the vihuela had fallen into some decline, and the guitar itself had another course added to make a total of five (ten strings). This instrument became known as the guitarra Espanola, and it enjoyed huge popularity across Europe, especially in the courts of France and Italy. The works of Spanish composer Gaspar Sanz (1640–1710), such as his *Galliardas*, *Canarios* and *Passacalles*, are among the most idiomatic and exciting for the then-new five-course instrument.

Other music from this period, such as the songs and instrumental music of British lutenist John Dowland, has become popular among modern guitarists as it transcribes quite well for the guitar. The "authentic instrument" movement has recently encouraged a great rise in the number of lute players, making the borrowing of repertoire less fashionable.

During the Baroque period the guitar gave up considerable ground to the harpsichord, Baroque lute and organ, which were the leading instruments. Although at the time composers like Boccherini wrote many works for guitar, especially some fine pieces with string quartet, a lot of the Baroque repertoire played on the guitar today was originally lute music – such as the four suites of JS Bach (1685–1750) and the sonatas of Leopold Weiss (1786–1750).

The transcription and performance of such repertoire appears less affected by current trends in Early music than that of Renaissance music. This is perhaps due to the smaller numbers of Baroque lutenists, and the fact that Bach's lute works, like much of his music, is less reliant on instrumental character for its effectiveness. The 'Prelude in D minor' is an ideal Bach piece for those seeking Baroque repertoire at the level reached by this book.

During the early part of the Classical period the guitar went

SECTION SIX
PLAY CLASSICAL GUITAR

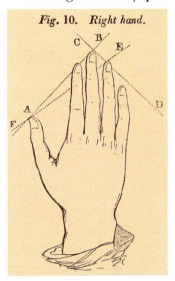
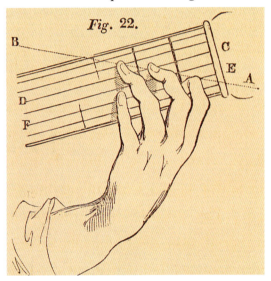

Illustrations from Fernando Sor's Method For The Spanish Guitar, showing the exact angles between the fingers to clarify playing position of the hands.

through a further physical change. Another bass course was added, and soon afterwards courses were dropped in favour of single strings, giving the standard six single strings as used to the present day. Although the instrument was still often referred to as the Spanish guitar, it had now become the classical guitar, and its clarity and sensitivity were well-suited to the new musical language forged by Haydn (1732–1809) and Mozart (1756–1791).

The main composers for the guitar at this time were the Catalan Fernando Sor (1778–1839), Spaniard Dionisio Aguado (1784–1849) and the Italian Maro Giuliani (1781–1828). Sor produced a significant amount of repertoire: both full-scale forms such as the 'Sonata in D' Opus 14 and many sets of *Variations*, one of the best-known being his 'Variations On A Theme Of Mozart'. Sor also wrote

SECTION SIX
PLAY CLASSICAL GUITAR

a large number of *etudes* (studies) dealing with various aspects of technique, and a number of very beautiful songs with guitar accompaniment. Aguado was famous for his brilliant technique and his *etudes* are invaluable in developing a thorough control of the instrument. As well as his solo works, Giuliani wrote a guitar concerto which displays a fine balance between the melodic and virtuosic aspects of the instrument. Other composers of this period include Carcassi, whose *etudes* provide good concert repertoire in their own right.

In the early to mid 19th century the guitar languished largely as a salon instrument. Constructional developments had increased the volume produced by both the piano and violin: these and an expansion in the musical language won over the majority of Romantic composers such as Liszt (1811–1886) and Paganini (1782–1840), though the latter did also write some guitar works and apparently played the instrument quite well. On top of this, the developments in opera by Wagner (1813–1883) served to focus the public's attention onto large-scale musical events. It took another physical change to the guitar before the instrument began to regain public favour.

The guitar-maker Antonio Torres (1817–92) revolutionised the instrument by developing a special strutting system to strengthen the soundboard (the guitar's resonating front panel) which resulted in a considerable increase in volume and tonal depth. The warm, sweet sound now produced by the treble strings greatly increased the scope for the melodic possibilities of the instrument. Guitarist and composer Francisco Tárrega (1852–1909) developed a new technique for playing the guitar in order to take full advantage of the potential of the new Torres instrument, and this forms the basis for the modern technique still used today.

A picture of early 19th century Spanish guitarist Dionisio Aguado, showing the unusual playing position he favoured for a time. He later came to use a special tripod stand to hold the instrument.

As a composer, Tárrega wrote many works which have since become classics of the repertoire. His best-known is probably the tremolo study 'Recuerdos De La Alhambra' ('Memories Of The Alhambra'). It was Andrés Segovia's recording of this piece which apparently inspired Julian Bream to become a guitarist. Tárrega's studies, sonatas and other pieces often deal with technical aspects of playing, but their foremost feature is a highly romantic melodic quality reminiscent of Chopin. Tárrega also transcribed a great deal of music from piano literature, especially that of his compatriot Albeniz. Tárrega's pupil Miguel Llobet (1878–1939) also made many transcriptions, ranging from arrangements of folk music to large-scale piano works. Interestingly, Llobet also transcribed the music of the vihuela for the modern guitar, leading to a growth in interest of this period among players and scholars.

The piano music of the Catalan composers Enrique Granados (1867–1916) and Isaac Albéniz (1860–1909), although often played by pianists, is highly suitable for the guitar. It not only transcribes well, but the sound of the instrument matches the language ideally, and one could easily believe many of their works are original guitar compositions. This is partly due to the nationalistic colour in their music, which makes use of native rhythms and themes originating in the folk use of the guitar. Particular examples are 'Leyenda' (also known as 'Asturias') by Albéniz and the 'Danza Españolas' and 'La Maja de Goya' by Granados.

Due to the incomparable efforts of Andrés Segovia (1893–1987) throughout the 20th century the guitar has now won international recognition as a serious instrument for the performance of Art music. Segovia's outstanding self-taught technique and musicianship quickly gave him the necessary status to commission large works

Francisco Tárrega playing a Torres instrument at the end of the 19th century. Note the right hand position, which is the basis for the modern technique.

SECTION SIX
PLAY CLASSICAL GUITAR

The great Andrés Segovia as a young man. It was then, at the very height of his virtuosity, that he began to gain international recognition.

specially written for the guitar. The first of these was the three-movement piece entitled 'Sonatina' by Federico Moreno Torroba (1891–1982). Other important works commissioned by Segovia are the 'Fandanguillo' by Turina and the 'Homenaje Pour Le Tombeau De Debussy' written by Manuel de Falla (1876–1946) to mark the death of Debussy (1862–1918). Following on from de Falla, Joaquín Rodrigo (1901–1999) became the most important Spanish composer of his time. Far from specialising in guitar music, he also wrote chamber and orchestra music. One of his greatest pieces is his solo guitar work 'Invocacion y Danza', a virtuosic piece with an almost Stravinskian opening. Rodrigo is best-known for his 'Concierto De Aranjuez', a full concerto for guitar and orchestra. Although somewhat Romantic in style, this is a masterwork with a highly demanding solo guitar part and subtle use of orchestration that allows the guitar to be clearly heard over the other instruments without amplification.

Outside Spain, and largely due to the international concert tours of the inexhaustible Segovia, music written for the guitar continued to grow in quality and quantity. In Brazil, Heitor Villa-Lobos (1887–1959) wrote 12 studies, five preludes and a concerto, making much use of his native rhythms. The four 'Venezuelan Dances' of Antonio Lauro (1917–1986) have also now entered the repertoire alongside the virtuosic pieces of the Paraguayan guitarist/composer

SECTION SIX
PLAY CLASSICAL GUITAR

British guitarist Julian Bream tirelessly undertook extensive concert tours and commissioned major works for the instrument, following the example set by Segovia. Bream himself has inspired two generations of UK guitarists to become concert players and recording artists.

Augustin Barrios Mangore (1885–1944). They received international attention due to the perfomance and recordings of their works by the Australian-born guitarist John Williams (b1941). British guitarist Julian Bream (b1933) continued the tradition of Segovia by commissioning composers of his own time, such as Benjamin Britten (1913–1976) and William Walton (1902–1983). The former's solo work for guitar, the 'Nocturnal', makes use of a song by John Dowland, subtly quoting the theme at the end of the piece. The 'Five Bagatelles' of Walton have become a favourite of many players, with their contrasting moods and use of Cuban rhythms. Major post-war composers such as Brian Ferneyhough (b1943) and Luciano Berio (b1925) have written solo pieces in the High Modernist language, further establishing the guitar's reputation by showing its ability to keep up with the latest developments in contemporary music.

Another side to the guitar repertoire which flourished in the 20th century came from its use in small mainstream ensembles (other than guitar duos and trios). The 'Drei Lieder' (1925) by Anton Webern (1883–1945) for soprano, clarinet and guitar is an early example, and the 'Marteau Sans Maitre' of Pierre Boulez (b1925) for alto voice and small ensemble is a major work making extensive use of the guitar. By the end of the 20th century one was as likely to find a guitar in a contemporary music ensemble as a piano – indicating its full emancipation after a rather chequered history.

SECTION SIX
PLAY CLASSICAL GUITAR

A guide to buying an instrument

Despite the traditional appearance, classical guitars come in a very wide variety of types and standards, and the choice can be slightly bewildering for the first-time buyer.

Although everyone wants to have a good sound, it must be remembered that tone quality depends as much on the player as it does on the instrument. Putting price and budget aside for a moment, a good general point is to try to match the level of the instrument with the level of your playing ability and experience. A good player will find a poor-quality instrument limiting and uneven in sound, while a beginner or first or second year student would make no use of the wide range of tone colour and volume that a high quality instrument offers.

A good instrument for a beginner can be had for between around £40 ($55) for Chinese-made guitars, and around £90 ($120) for Spanish-made.

A very important initial decision concerns the size of the guitar. If it's a young child who is learning, between say five and eight years old, then a half-size instrument would be suitable. Although height and hand-size vary greatly, for a child around nine or ten years old a ⅞ size guitar should be considered. From 14 or 15 upwards, most people would be better off with a full-size instrument. The only way to be really sure is to have the child hold the instrument in the correct position: if he or she has difficulty reaching over the body to the strings with the right arm, and/or can't reach the first fret without straightening the left arm, then a smaller sized guitar might be better.

The size of a guitar is often described by its scale length, which is the distance from the nut to the bridge. The standard full-size is 650mm, and the ⅞ scale is around 640mm. There was a period in the 1980s when larger instruments were made, with a length of 657mm, but they often proved unwieldy (except for players with very large hands) and they are rare nowadays.

Ideally, if a student is very serious about learning the guitar and expects to spend some years devoted to it, an instrument with a certain amount of room for development would be the best choice. This will probably mean purchasing a guitar of average capability, with a solid top (soundboard), for which you might expect to pay around £140 ($190).

Going up slightly in price, you'll find guitars using better quality timber for the back and sides, which adds significantly to the definition of the tone. It's also around this price range that you'll start to see hand-made instruments. But the soundboard is the most important element as far as sound and projection are concerned (see fold-out page for guitar construction details). The choice of spruce or cedar top is directly related to the kind of sound required, and also to the type of repertoire you intend to play (although this will only be a consideration for more accomplished players). Generally speaking, cedar-top guitars usually have a slightly warmer sound than spruce tops, but remember that the overall quality of the instrument can heavily outweigh this factor. The use of spruce gives a slightly more focused sound and is well-suited to contrapuntal music such as

Centre and right: 1974 Masaru Kohno guitar, with spruce top and Brazillian rosewood back and sides.
Left: 1967 Ramirez 3 Madrid (type 1a concert classical guitar) with western red cedar top.

SECTION SIX
PLAY CLASSICAL GUITAR

Renaissance and Baroque repertoire and ensemble playing. Having said all this, the number of variables in guitar construction is so enormous that each instrument must be taken on its own merits. The size of the body also plays a major role in the focus of the sound – although a big body is not always louder, as the tone can become diffused. What appears to be volume is not necessarily true projection, which is what's required to reach the back of a concert hall.

As a player reaches the level where a more expensive instrument is needed, personal preference and experience will be the deciding factors. In the mid-range of prices you might pay around £500-800 ($700-1,100). There are many extremely good makers, and it's advisable to take your time, and play as many instruments as possible. Try talking to guitar students at a college or university – they may even be in the market to sell their own mid-range instrument as they begin to prepare for a professional playing career. Professional concert instruments can be priced from around £1,000 ($1,400) upwards to about £4,000 ($5,600). Guitars tend to level off around this price – those costing more usually do so because of historical associations. At this elevated level you might be buying a guitar that once belonged to Julian Bream, or a rare example from a guitar-maker no longer working.

These pictures show some of the more important woods used in guitar-making: the top line has four soundboards, and the bottom line shows guitar backs where cosmetic factors are more relevant.

1 European spruce
2 Hakkaido spruce
3 Western red cedar
4 Western red cedar with a matt finish
5 Cypress
6 Brazillian rosewood
7 more Brazillian rosewood
8 Indian rosewood

Accelerando (acc) Speeding up.
Accent A stress on a particular note, to change or highlight the rhythmic emphasis of a bar.
Acciaccatura A very fast, "crushed in" note before the main one; an example of an ornament or grace note.
Accidental A sharp, flat or natural sign next to an individual note, changing its pitch by a semitone, and cancelled by the next bar line.
Action Height of the strings above fingerboard.
Adagio At ease, slow (less slow than largo).
Aleatorism The use of chance in composition or performance (from the Latin word alea, meaning dice); initiated by John Cage (1912–1992).
Allegro Lively, merry.
Alphabeto A 17th century Italian notation system using an alphabet of chord symbols.
Anacrusis An upbeat before the first proper bar of music.
Andante Moving along at a walking pace.
Anular Ring (third) finger of right hand; abbreviated to **a**.
Apoyando A right-hand technique, also known as the rest stroke, in which the playing finger passes "through" the string, coming to rest on the adjacent string.
Appoggiatura Leaning note; a grace note lasting half the length of the note it precedes.
Arpeggio A broken chord, in which the notes are played sequentially rather than together.

Arrangement Adaptation of music written for other instruments so it can be played on the guitar. It may also be called transcription.
A tempo Revert to previous speed after a deviation.
Atonal A type of composition, usually written since the start of the 19th century, which has no allegiance to a tonal centre.
Bandurría Spanish folk instrument with a pear-shaped body and steel strings.
Bar A regular rhythmic measure; music is visually divided up by the insertion of vertical "bar lines" on the stave – single lines between each measure, double lines at the end of the piece.
Barre Several notes held down by one finger stretched partly (half-barre) or entirely (full-barre) across the neck at one fret.
Bartók See Snap pizz.
Bass The lower-pitched part(s) of a piece of music, which give it harmonic foundation.
Belly Another name for the soundboard of the guitar.
Binding A continuous strip of wood or other material fitted to the outer edge of a guitar body for decorative purposes.
Bi-tonality The use of two keys simultaneously; used widely by Stravinsky (1882–1971).
Bookmatched Decorative effect made from a piece of wood split into two sheets and joined with the grain matching symmetrically.
Bordón or Bourdon Lowest string on an early guitar.
Bossa nova A musical style derived from the influence of West Coast jazz upon Brazilian samba rhythms.
Bout Upper or lower section of the guitar body.
Braces Wooden structures beneath guitar front and back intended to enhance strength and tonal response.
Bracing The pattern of braces used inside a guitar's body.
Brazilian rosewood Tropical hardwood formerly used in the making of guitar bodies. Now a protected species.
Bridge Rectangular block of wood to which strings are attached, usually by tying.
Bridge-block The drilled section of the bridge through which the strings are threaded.
Bridge plate Flat plate on the guitar's soundboard beneath the bridge. It is favoured by some builders who make it part of their strutting pattern.
Button Decorative and practical knob used to turn machineheads.
Cadenza A virtuosic solo passage, usually in a concerto and sometimes improvised.
Campanella "Little bell"; use of ringing open strings to create bell-like sound.
Cantabile Voice-like, or with a singing quality.
Capo (capo tasto, capo dastro) A movable device for clamping the strings at a particular fret to raise the guitar's pitch.
Cedar Evergreen conifer used particularly for guitar necks.
Chitarra battente Steel-strung guitar used in the popular music

of 18th century Italy.

Chord A combination of three or more notes played at the same time; also used to describe the "prepared" right-hand fingering position on the strings.

Chromatic A scale using all 12 semitones within an octave.

Clef Symbol usually at the start of each line of music, fixing the exact pitch of notes on the stave; the most commonly used are the treble clef and bass clef.

Cittern Small, flat pear-shaped instrument with metal strings, popular in Europe from the middle ages to the 18th century; not the same as gittern.

Common time Four crotchets (quarter-notes) in a bar; abbreviated to C.

Con brio With spirit, vigour.

Concert guitar Guitar intended for the public performance of so-called Art music.

Concert study An extended study, or étude, often with considerable musical value.

Concerto An extended work that features a solo instrument and an orchestra.

Consonance Combination of conventionally pleasing sounds (in the classic tonal system); opposite of dissonance.

Continuo Music improvised over a written bass part; it is commonly found in Baroque and early Classical works.

Contour The shape of a melody or theme expressed in terms of the shifts in pitch.

Counterpoint Music made up of two or more independent melody lines, moving "horizontally"; the adjective is contrapuntal.

Coupling Exchange of mechanical energy between string and soundboard.

Course A pair of strings tuned in unison or an octave apart, as used in Baroque guitars.

Crescendo Getting louder.

Crotchet Quarter-note; one quarter the length of a semibreve (whole-note).

Cypress A conifer used in the 19th century for the bodies of cheaper guitars, and later flamenco instruments.

Damping Stopping a note ringing out by touching it with a finger or thumb.

Demisemiquaver 32nd-note.

Despacio Slowly.

Diatonic Scales using selected notes in an octave (eg major, minor scale, etc).

Diminuendo Getting quieter.

Dissonance A sound produced by non-consonant intervals played together.

Dolce Sweet, soft.

Domed Describing a soundboard that is arched both longitudinally and transversely.

Dominant Fifth degree of a major or minor scale; five notes higher than the tonic (including the tonic note when counting).

Dot A dot after a note increases its length by half.

Doubling Adding more of the same notes to fill out the sound of a chord triad.

Dynamics Changes in volume throughout a piece of music.

Eighth-note Quaver; one eighth of a whole-note (semibreve).

End-block Thick wooden block used to join sides of guitar at the lower bout.

English guitar An 18th century version of the cittern.

Enharmonic Two notes, or intervals, sounding the same even if their names are different.

Étude or Study Piece intended to help players develop their technical skills; often of some musical value in itself.

European spruce Wood used for soundboards; spruce originally meant "from Prussia".

Extended techniques Unusual playing practices outside the "normal" use of the instrument.

Fan-strutting Wooden struts on underside of soundboard, arranged rather like an open fan.

Fantasia (16th century) contrapuntal piece; (19th century) poetic, allusive piece with no fixed form.

Fermata Pause.

Fine End, in Italian.

Fingerboard The hard playing surface glued to the neck to carry the frets; usually made of ebony or rosewood.

Flat A sign lowering a note by one semitone.

Foot Part of the neck which extends inside the body.

Form The overall structure or architecture of a piece of music (the order that passages are played, repeated etc).

Forte Loud.

French polishing A traditional varnishing technique where shellac dissolved in alcohol is

rubbed into wood.
Fret Metal strip across fingerboard used to determine pitch; ivory or gut were used on early instruments.
Fretboard The fingerboard.
Friction peg Traditional tuning peg held in position by friction of wood in hole. Now only on flamenco guitars.
Gittern Small gut-strung lute of the Renaissance era. It was formerly considered to be an ancestor of the guitar.
Glissando A clearly audible slide from one note to another (similar to portamento on unfretted instruments); abbreviated to gliss.
Glue-blocks Small wooden blocks used to glue top and back of guitar to sides.
Guitarrero Guitar maker.
Guitarrista Guitarist.
Gumi-laca This is the Spanish name for the natural lacquer used in French polishing.
Grave Slow and solemn.
Gut Name for the cured animal intestines used for strings before the development of nylon.
Hairpin Dynamic markings on the stave.
Half-note Minim; half the length of a whole-note (semibreve).
Harmonic bar Reinforcing bar glued to the inside of the soundboard across the body of the guitar.
Harmonics Overtones, or higher frequency sounds, generated at the same time as any fundamental note. Heard on the guitar by touching the string at strategic points to damp the fundamental.

Harmony Simultaneous combining of notes "vertically" (often as chords) to complement but not compete with the main melody. (Can be contrasted with counterpoint.)
Head Extension of the neck, holding machineheads.
Heel Exterior part of the neck-block to which the guitar sides are fitted.
Hemidemisemiquaver British term for 64th-note.
Indian rosewood Tropical evergreen hardwood, used in making guitar bodies, especially now Brazilian rosewood is not freely available.
Indice Index (first) finger of right hand; abbreviated to **i**.
Interval The difference – that is to say the distance in pitch – between two notes.
Irrational rhythms Irregular rhythmic groupings, also known as tuplets; squeezing more notes into a beat than the time signature dictates.
Kerfed lining Strip of wood with notches to make it flexible enough to follow the shape of the guitar's sides.
Key signature A number of sharps or flats noted at the start indicating the tonal centre on which a piece is based.
Lacquer A traditional finish for guitars, usually hand-applied over a long period.
Largo Broad, slow, dignified.
Laud Small Spanish folk instrument with metal strings.
Ledger lines Short lines added above or below the stave to

accommodate high or low notes.
Legato Smoothly.
Lento Slow.
Ligado Slur; technique where the left-hand plays the strings by hammering on and pulling off.
Line The melody or tune in a piece of music.
Lining A continuous strip of wood used to join guitar sides to top and back.
Lower bout Section of guitar body below the waist.
Lute Medieval and Renaissance musical instrument.
Luthier Instrument builder; originally lute-maker.
Machineheads Mechanical gears for altering string tension and consequently pitch.
Measure Another (mainly US) word for bar.
Medio Middle (second) finger of right hand; abbreviated to **m**.
Meno Less.
Metronome Clockwork device for counting beats and keeping time; patented by Maelzel during the early 19th century.
Mezzo Moderate strength.
Minim Half-note; half the length of a semibreve (whole-note).
Modality The use of a mode to produce harmony and line; it was common in the middle ages as well as the Renaissance, and in much folk music.
Mode A scale with a particular set and order of intervals.
Moderato Means "moderate", and thus is similar to andante.
Modes of vibration The different types of movement in any vibrating body.

Molto Very (Italian term).
Mordent Ornament played as a three-note slur and used to emphasise a note.
Mosso Movement, speed.
Mother-of-pearl Shell of some molluscs, used for decoration of rosettes, tuning pegs etc.
Motif A short musical phrase, usually repeated and developed in a piece.
Natural A note that is neither sharpened nor flattened.
Neck-block The end of the neck as it meets the body, built up to join to sides, top and back.
Nocturne A piece relating to night and its associations.
Node A stationary part of a vibrating body; used to produce harmonics on strings.
Notation The various methods of writing down music.
Note A single sound, which has pitch and length. In US often called a tone.
Note value The length, and name, of the note unit; for example a crotchet (quarter-note), minim (half-note), quaver (eighth-note) and so on.
Nut Bar of ivory or bone determining string spacing and height at head-end of neck.
Octave An interval of eight notes, including first and last, joining two notes of the same name; each octave is in fact made up of 12 semitones, different combinations of which make up different scales.
Ornament Decoration or embellishment of note or phrase, indicated by small symbols or letters on the stave.
Pentatonic A scale containing only five notes, popular in Western and Oriental folk music.
Piano In written music this term means soft, or quiet.
Pin bridge A bridge that secures the strings in place by pins rather than by tying.
Pitch Sonic frequency of a note – how high or low it sounds, and where the note fits on a scale.
Più More.
Pizzicato Guitar technique using the right hand to damp the strings while plucking with the thumb, reproducing the sound of a plucked violin/cello.
Plantilla Spanish term for the outline of a guitar body.
Plate Scientific term for the vibrating soundboard.
Plectrum Small object held in right hand to strike strings.
Poco A little.
Polyphonic Music made up of several independent lines, known as voices.
Portamento A clearly audible slide from one note to another (on the guitar this is more properly called glissando).
Position Left-hand placement centred on particular frets, allowing access to a certain group of notes; first position is at the first fret, nearest the nut.
Prelude Originally the opening piece of a set, but since 19th century preludes no longer have to precede, and are often written as one-movement pieces.
Presto Quick (Italian term).
Pulgar Thumb, abbreviated to **p**.
Punteado The plucking of individual notes.
Purfling Decorative inlays around the perimeter of the guitar alongside the binding.
Quarter-note Crotchet; a quarter of a semibreve (whole note).
Quaver Eighth-note; an eighth of the length of a semibreve (whole note); one half the length of a crotchet.
Rallentando Slowing down gradually; abbreviated to rall.
Rasguedo Strumming, especially using the back of the fingers.
Repertoire Body of work written for a particular instrument or played by particular musicians.
Resonant frequency The frequency at which any object is likely to vibrate most with the least stimulation.
Rest A silence or pause in the music, and the notation for this.
Rib-block A wooden block inside the guitar body used to support its harmonic and transverse bars.
Ribs The sides of the guitar.
Ritardo Delayed, held-back; abbreviated to rit.
Rose Intricate fretted wood or parchment covering for soundhole in early guitars.
Rosette Intricate decoration around soundhole, usually in marquetry or wood mosaic.
Rosewood Hardwood used for guitar fingerboards and bodies; see Indian/Brazilian.
Rubato "Robbed time", where strict tempo is interrupted briefly to accentuate a certain phrase.
Saddle This is a strip of bone, ivory or other material over which

the strings pass at the bridge.
Samba Brazilian dance with African origins.
Scale A series of individual notes, going up or down.
Scale length The distance from a guitar nut to 12th fret, multiplied by two.
Scordatura Deliberate re-tuning of one or more strings.
Score The musical notation of an entire piece for a performer to play from.
Semibreve Whole-note.
Semiquaver 16th-note; quarter of a crotchet; 16th of a semibreve (whole note).
Sempre Always; all through a piece unless cancelled by a contrary instruction.
Sequences Repetitions of a motif at different pitches, or varying intervals, but keeping the same rhythm. This is common in Baroque music.
Serialism Post-19th century alternative to traditional tonal system, where all 12 intervals are considered equal (no dominant, tonic etc), and in which the music is governed by a set order of the notes.
Sforzando Accented.
Sharp A sign raising a note by one semitone.
Shellac A natural thermoplastic resin made from the secretions of the Asian lac insect.
16th-note Semiquaver; one 16th the length of a semibreve (whole note); one quarter of a crotchet.
64th-note Hemidemisemiquaver.
Slur A smooth, seamless left-hand change between notes of different pitch.
Snap pizz Technique (credited to Béla Bartók) where a string is pulled away from the fingerboard and allowed to snap back.
Soloist A performer who plays solo, either entirely alone or within an ensemble.
Soundboard The vibrating top (front) surface of a guitar body.
Soundhole Hole in soundboard to facilitate sound projection.
Splice-joint One method of fixing head to neck.
Spruce A coniferous tree, used for soundboard wood.
Staff See stave.
Stave Five parallel lines where music is notated; also sometimes called a staff.
String-block The drilled section of a bridge through which the strings are threaded.
String length Sounding length of string, measured from nut to bridge saddle.
Struts Wood structures beneath guitar front and back to enhance strength and tonal response.
Strutting The pattern of struts used inside a guitar's body.
Study or Étude Piece intended for teaching purposes, sometimes also of musical value.
Suite A group of pieces based on dance forms.
Sympathetic resonance Sound produced by open strings that are not struck.
Syncopation Displacement of the normal beat.
Tablature System of musical notation indicating the position of the fingers on frets and strings (sometimes abbreviated to Tab).
Table Another name for the soundboard or top of a guitar.
Tambor Using the thumb to strike the strings near the bridge, for percussive effect; from the Spanish word for drum.
Tango Argentinian dance related to the Cuban habañera and probably of African origin.
Tapa Spanish word for soundboard (literally "the lid").
Tempo The speed of a piece of music. Tempo is generally notated as a number of beats per minute; this is known as a Metronome Mark (MM).
Theorbo A type of large lute.
32nd-note Demisemiquaver.
Tie Curved line on stave between two notes of the same pitch; the second note isn't played, just held for the length of its note value.
Timbre Tone colour; the quality of a sound.
Time signature Numbers or symbols at the start of a written piece (after the clef and key signature) indicating the time, or metre, of the music; eg 6 over 8 indicates six quavers (quarter-notes) to a bar.
Tirando Right-hand technique also known as the free stroke, in which the playing finger plucks the string but does not make contact with the adjacent string.
Tonal system The standard Western "classical" organisation of music, based around keys and their interrelationships.
Tone Mainly US word for note; also, generally, the quality or timbre of a musical sound.

Tonewood Wood used in the making of musical instruments.
Tonic The key note; first note of a major or minor scale.
Top The soundboard, also known as the table.
Tornavoz Metal cylinder inside soundhole intended to aid projection; used by Torres but now scorned.
Turn Short pattern of four notes making a little flourish into the next note.
Tranquillo Tranquil, peaceful.
Transcription Adaptation of music written for other instruments so it can be played on the guitar. The result may also be called an arrangement.
Transverse bar Bar glued across the back inside the guitar's body.
Treble The upper part(s) in music; usually providing the theme and melody.
Tremolo Rapid repetition of note using right-hand fingers to give impression of longer sustain.
Triad A particular combination of three notes forming the basis of a chord.
Trill Extended alternation between main note and the one above it, played as a seamless series of left-hand slurs.
Triple time Three beats in a bar; 3 over 4 means three crotchets per measure.
Triplet Three notes that are played in the time it normally takes to play two.
Tuning pegs Machineheads or friction pegs.
'Ud Arabic instrument introduced into Spain by the Moors, with important consequences for lute making.
Upper bout Section of guitar body above waist.
Variations Embellishments of a musical theme.
Varnish Protective and decorative surface applied to guitar bodies; shellac, man-made urethane etc.
Vibrato Subtle side-to-side finger movement on the fretboard that produces slight pitch fluctuation.
Vihuela Spanish instrument of the 15th & 16th centuries, resembling the guitar but musically closer to the lute.
Vihuela de mano Version of the vihuela plucked with fingers rather than a quill or plectrum.
Virtuoso An instrumental performer with excellent technical and musical abilities.
Vivace Vivacious, full of life.
V-joint One of the methods of fixing head to neck or neck to body. It is more complex than a normal splice-joint.
Waist The narrowest part of the guitar body.
Waisted Guitar body with figure-of-eight shape.
Western red cedar Not a cedar, but a conifer now used by many guitar-makers.
Whole-note Semibreve.
Wolf note On stringed instruments, a note with a sound unpleasantly different from those around it; a phenomenon much affected by guitar construction.

DAVID BRAID has taught classical guitar for many years and has worked internationally as a solo and chamber performer. He studied the guitar privately in North Wales with Jonathan Richards, progressing to London's Royal College Of Music in 1990 where he studied guitar with Charles Ramirez and composition with Edwin Roxburgh. After post-graduate study in composition at the Krakow Academy Of Music in Poland, David returned to the Royal College in 1997 and completed his Masters Degree in composition. His work has been played in Denmark, Germany, Poland, Spain, Sweden and the UK. He writes about many aspects of music, and is a contributor to the *Music In The 20th Century* encyclopedia. David's awards include the Jack Morrison Prize for guitar, the Accessit prize for youth orchestra composition, and the Chameleon Composers' Group prize.

AUDIO CD INSTRUCTIONS
The tracks on the CD relate directly to the exercise numbers throughout this book. For example, if you want to hear David Braid play exercise 23, key in track 23 on your CD player. The exceptions are the four study pieces: Study Piece 1 is track 93; Study Piece 2 is track 94; Study Piece 3 is track 95; and Study Piece 4 is track 96.